conversations
you *must* have with
your son

5
conversations
you *must* have with
your **son**

Vicki
Courtney

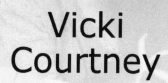

PUBLISHING GROUP

www.BHPublishingGroup.com

978-0-8054-4986-0

Published by B&H Publishing Group

Nashville, Tennessee

Dewey Decimal Classification: 306.874

Subject Heading: BOYS \ PARENT AND CHILD \

PARENTING

Author is represented by Alive Communications, Inc., 7680 Goddard Street, Suite 200, Colorado Springs, CO 80920.

Unless otherwise noted, Scripture quotations are from the Holy Bible, New International Version, copyright © 1973, 1978, 1984 by International Bible Society. Other versions include: New Living Translation (NLT), copyright © 1996. Used by permission of Tyndale House Publishers, Inc., Wheaton, IL 60189 USA. All rights reserved.; English Standard Version (ESV), copyright © 2001 by Crossway Bibles, a ministry of the Good News Publishers of Wheaton, IL; and The King James Version (KJV).

4 5 6 7 8 9 10 • 16 15 14 13 12 11

*D*edication

To my sons, Ryan and Hayden—
Thank you for patiently enduring the conversations contained
in this book (or at least pretending to!). One of my greatest joys in
life has been raising you two boys from the cradle to college.
I love you!

Acknowledgments

Keith, I continue to acknowledge and thank you in every book, but it bears repeating: I could not do what I do were it not for you picking up the slack (and countless to-go meals!). Thank you also for contributing the Dad:2:Dad bonus material for the 5 Conversations blog. As I read through it, I was struck with how purposeful you have been in discipling our sons over the years. Truly you should be the one writing this book . . . or at least, one to follow for dads, perhaps? Our sons (and daughter) are so very blessed to have you for a dad. And I am even more blessed to have you for my own. Empty nest years, here we come!

Ryan and Hayden, when you were wee little lads, I would often tell you, while tucking you in at night during our bedtime prayers: *"I'm so glad God picked me to be your mama."* I mean it more today than ever before. I'm so glad God picked me to be your mama! I am so very proud of you both and the heart you have for the Lord. I cannot wait to see what He has in store for you in the future. Devote your lives to living for Him and you can't go wrong.

viii 5 CONVERSATIONS YOU *must* HAVE WITH YOUR SON

Matt, at the time I am writing the acknowledgements for this book, you are a few weeks shy of proposing to my daughter. When you called her dad and asked for our daughter's hand in marriage, we were beside ourselves with excitement. You are exactly what we pictured all these years when we prayed for our daughter's future husband. Welcome to the family, son!

Lee, every book I write will include a thank-you and a shout-out to my amazing agent, which basically means you cannot retire until I've written my last and final book. Deal?

Jennifer Lyell and B&H crew, thank you so much for partnering with me to get this message out to moms with sons. I feel certain the next title in this series should be *5 Conversations You Must Have with Your Yorkies*, since I talk nonstop to my pups throughout the day. Let's talk about it . . . there are lots of dog lovers out there!

To my blog readers with sons who have encouraged me to write this book, cheered me on in the process, and helped out by answering the many questions I've asked about your own parenting journeys: Thank you so much for your support. Your sons are blessed to have such caring and concerned mothers.

And last of all, the acknowledgments would not be complete without giving thanks to the one who enables me to write, speak, live, breathe, and love. I pray this book will bring glory and honor to my Savior, Jesus Christ.

$\mathcal{C}$ontents

Introduction

As with most of the introductions I've written for past books, I save this task for last. I'm always mindful of the fact that the introduction acts as a first impression for a reader. Therefore I want you to know right up front that I'm not an expert on raising boys. I hold no degrees in childhood development, and I cringe inside when someone mistakenly introduces me as a "teen culture expert," which has been known to happen on occasion. I'm just a mom in the trenches like you, who loves her boys to pieces and desperately wants what's best for them.

When I brought my oldest son home from the hospital, I was at a complete loss as to how to raise a boy. Having a younger brother had given me a small taste of the wonderful world of boys, so I wasn't completely ignorant to common boy antics (like their fascination with belching, passing gas, and talking non-stop about belching and passing gas). When I looked at my precious, innocent newborn son, I had a few flashbacks of some of my brother's testosterone-fueled adventures and felt a shiver go up my spine. Let's see . . . there was the time he jumped off the roof into a pile of leaves, insisting to his friends it would cushion his fall. For the record, it didn't. Or the time he and a neighbor kid set an abandoned house on fire, and a team of firemen came to our front door to question him (he was hiding in his closet). And who could forget the time he shot me (accidentally) in the fingernail with a BB gun? But the worst memory by far is being forced to share a bathroom with him. (This served as a contributing factor to my daughter getting her own bathroom when we built our house. Enough said.) Two sons later I'm still not quite sure I understand the world of boys any better than I did on the day it all began. Yet hundreds of mildewed socks and tinkled-on-toilet-seats later, I am completely smitten. My boys have stolen my heart. I have a hunch you feel the same way or you probably wouldn't have picked up this book.

You might have noted that the subtitle of this book is *From the cradle to college . . . telling your son the truth about life before he believes the culture's lies.*

I have kept you in mind as I've written this book, ever mindful that some of you have sons closer to the cradle season of life, and yet others, like me, have sons closer to the college season of life. Several years ago when I wrote *5 Conversations You Must Have with Your Daughter*, I did so in my only daughter's senior year of high school. The book released within a month of dropping her off at college (out of state), which made the timing rather ironic. I noted the irony of the timing in the introduction of that book, and yet, here I am again experiencing the same ironic timing. During the course of writing this book, here are a few things I have marked through on my to-do list:

- Attended my youngest son's last-ever high school football game.
- Written checks for my youngest son's senior pictures, graduation invitations, and cap and gown.
- Helped my youngest son apply to colleges and celebrated his decision to attend The University of Texas.
- Celebrated my oldest son's college graduation (Auburn University) and moved him back to his hometown of Austin, Texas.
- Celebrated my oldest son getting his first "real job" and being officially OFF OUR PAYROLL!!
- Celebrated my oldest son's engagement and marriage to a wonderful Christian young lady.

Who would have ever guessed that the timing of the release of this book would coincide with the end of my own sons' cradle to college journeys?! And as if that isn't surreal enough, add to the list:

- Colluded with my daughter's boyfriend (a wonderful Christian young man) to help him come up with the perfect engagement ring and a creative proposal idea.

By the time this book hits the shelves, my oldest son will be married, my youngest son will be packing for college, and my daughter will be preparing to walk down the aisle and say, "I do." Oh, and did I mention that my husband and I will become official "empty-nesters" in the middle of the whirlwind of events? It has been a year filled with emotional whiplash moments as we mourn a long list of last-evers and celebrate many first-evers.

Needless to say, the conversations I've discussed in this book have been ever present on my mind as I've been reminded firsthand of how quickly time flies. Please know that my children are far from perfect. My husband and I have experienced bumps along the way and oftentimes felt like we were learning as we go. In fact, I just recently told a friend that I finally feel like I'm getting this parenting thing down, and lo and behold here I am at the end of the journey! There is no foolproof formula when it comes to raising children who love the Lord and abide by His truths. Sometimes we will see immediate fruit from the holy deposits we make in our children's lives; while other times, it may not be until many years later. And yet other times it may not be until those grandchildren come along and our children gain a sudden appreciation for the responsibilities that come with parenting!

As I've reflected on my own parenting journey, I've rested in the peace that I am only responsible for the role I play. Ultimately I have no control over the results. As my husband and I begin a new chapter in our parenting journey, we will talk less when it comes to the conversations presented in this book—and pray more. Most important, we will rest in a settled peace that we have taken advantage of teachable moments (Deut. 6:6–9) and had many conversations with our children along the way. What they do with that investment will in the end be up to our children. Parenting is hard work, but I wouldn't trade the journey for anything. Whether the reward for your hard work is immediate or delayed, I'm sure you echo the sentiments of 3 John 4 when it says, "Truly, I have no greater joy than to hear that my children are walking in the truth." Persevere. Hold out for the prize. Do your part by making holy deposits in your sons' lives. And trust God for the results.

CONVERSATION 1

*Don't define manhood by
the culture's wimpy standards.
It's OK to be a man!*

CHAPTER 1

The Wimpification of the Modern Male

The natives are restless. And by natives I mean the men of America, the *real* men who value their masculinity and have decided to rise up and reclaim it. After years spent attempting to tame their testosterone in order to fit the feminized mold of manhood as defined by popular opinion, they've had enough. The Marlboro Man (minus the cancer stick affixed in the corner of his mouth) is making a comeback, and I can assure you he won't be stopping by Starbucks for an iced caramel frappuccino on his way into town. If ever there was evidence of a growing resurgence to reclaim manhood, it could be found in the Super Bowl ads that aired during the game while I was in the process of outlining this book.

First, there was a commercial where CBS's Jim Nantz delivered an "injury report" on a guy (Jason) whose girlfriend has "removed his spine." Microphone in hand, Jim delivers his lines in newscaster fashion as Jason is forced to shop with his girlfriend during game time. The first scene shows poor Jason standing in a lingerie shop with a red bra draped over his shoulder staring in a catatonic gaze as his girlfriend flips through the sales rack in the background. The ad is for FLO-TV, which would allow Jason to watch the game on his mobile phone. Voila, problem solved for the army of emasculated men who were fortunate enough to be tuning into the Super Bowl game from their living rooms with their buddies and a platter of buffalo wings. I imagine there was a chorus of high-fives among game watchers when Jim Nantz delivered the final line in the ad: "Change out of that skirt, Jason."[1]

And then there was the Dockers "Men without Pants" thirty-second ad spot that addressed the emasculated state of manhood by showing a group of childish men marching in a field (pantless) and singing, "I wear no pants." They were interrupted with the message: "Calling all men, it's time to wear the pants."

Jen Sey, vice president of Dockers global marketing commented, "We're sending out a humorous call to manhood . . . The campaign celebrates the reemergence of the khaki, a product whose heritage is rooted in the military, as an everyday way for men to convey masculine pride." She added that the message in the ad is for men to "wear the pants" both literally and figuratively.[2]

But perhaps the most misogynistic ad of the bunch was an ad for Dodge. It showed a series of men who stared into the camera lens with a hollow and expressionless look on their faces as the laundry list of male indignities (doled out by women) were listed one by one by a narrator.

- I will get up and walk the dog at 6:20 a.m.
- I will eat some fruit as part of my breakfast.
- I will shave, clean the sink after I shave.
- I will be at work at 8:00 a.m.
- I will sit through two-hour meetings.
- I will say yes when you want me to say yes.
- I will be quiet when you don't want me to say no.
- I will take your call and listen to your opinion of my friends.
- I will listen to your friends' opinions of my friends.
- I will be civil to your mother.
- I will put the seat down.
- I will separate the recycling.
- I will carry your lip-balm.
- I will watch your vampire TV shows with you.
- I will take my socks off before getting into bed.
- I will put my underwear in the basket.

The narrator's tone began with an edge of quiet confidence that by the end of the ad turned into raw anger as it culminated with the line, "And because I do this. I will drive the car, I want to drive. Charger, Man's Last Stand."[3]

The ads were intended to garner a laugh and, of course, to sell products. But don't be fooled; something much deeper was going on in the thirty-second ad spots. At the risk of alienating their female audience, the advertisers publicly acknowledged the burgeoning identity crisis regarding manhood and the shame that has resulted. The advertisers ponied up big bucks to identify with the emasculated male and, in a sense, give him permission to revolt. In front of an estimated 106 million viewers, it was as if they shook a collective burly knuckled fist (no buffed nails on these manly hands) into the face of radical feminism. By publicly addressing the identity crisis facing manhood (in a humorous fashion), they said in thirty seconds what many of us have been thinking for years. I couldn't help but get a visual picture in my mind of men across America joining in on a Twisted Sisters anthem, "Oh we're not gonna take it; no, we ain't gonna take it; oh we're not gonna take it anymore!"

In *Wild at Heart* author John Eldredge sums up the challenge our boys face: "Society at large can't make up its mind about men. Having spent the last thirty years redefining masculinity into something more sensitive, safe, manageable and, well, feminine, it now berates men for not being men."[4] First Chronicles 12:22 speaks of the men of Issachar who "understood the temper of the times and knew the best course for Israel to take." As mothers, we will be one of the strongest voices in our sons' lives. Like the men of Issachar, we too must understand the temper of the times and determine the best course to take when it comes to raising our sons to model biblical manhood.

I don't know about you, but I'm not one to sit on the sidelines in a spirit of defeat and point the finger of blame over the current state of manhood. I have a feeling you're probably a lot like me or you likely wouldn't have picked up this book. Rather than dwell in depth on how we got here, I would rather focus the conversation on where we go from here. In other words, what are the solutions? Again, only in understanding the temper of the times will we be able to come up with an effective game plan and move forward.

> *As mothers, we will be one of the strongest voices in our sons' lives.*

The Androgynous Blurring of the Lines

If we are to raise our boys to be the men God intended, then we must first acknowledge that while we were all created in God's image, there are distinct differences in the makeup of males and females. I imagine I'm preaching to the choir on this point, but I want to make sure we don't become desensitized to this truth. In an excellent article entitled, "Is America Still Making Men?" author Dennis Prager lists key factors that have contributed over the years to the lack of "real men" in our society today. Coming in at number 3 on his list is, "The ideals of masculinity and femininity have been largely rendered extinct." Prager further says, "Feminism, arguably the most influential American movement of the twentieth-century, declared war on the concepts of femininity and masculinity. And for much of the population, it was victorious. Indeed, thanks to the feminist teaching that male and female human beings are essentially the same (note, incidentally, that no one argues that male and female animals are the same, only human beings are), untold numbers of boys have been raised as if they were like girls."[5]

While thumbing through a sales catalog I received in the mail from the maker of a popular line of teen furnishings, I recently ran across an extreme example of the fallout from the androgyny movement. My eyes rested on one particular image that included several teen models. A girl was sitting on a furry, neon-colored beanbag chair. Standing within a few feet of her was a guy, smiling and gesticulating as though engaged in conversation. And next to him was another guy. Or wait, was it a girl? The model had short hair and wore skinny jeans and a baggy button shirt. He/she was lanky with androgynous facial features that appeared neither overtly masculine nor feminine. I looked for any hint that might tip the scale in one direction, but I finally gave up. I felt unsettled over the image of the he/she model, but sadly I wasn't surprised, given the times.

If you look up the word *androgyny* in the dictionary, you might find the following definition:

Androgynous (adjective)

1. being both male and female; hermaphroditic.
2. having both masculine and feminine characteristics.
3. having an ambiguous sexual identity.
4. neither clearly masculine nor clearly feminine in appearance: the androgynous look of many rock stars.[6]

Consider the following comment I found on an online forum discussing the androgynous fashion trend: "Androgyny is in, and it's about time!" The fashion industry correctly predicted current trends over thirty years ago with the unisex style and continued to capitalize on the popularity of androgynous dress, copying the styles of Boy George and Michael Jackson." Oh boy. Just what every mother of a son wants for her boy, to raise him to emulate the look and likeness of Boy George and Michael Jackson. It's one thing to share clothes with my daughter, but if one of my boys raids my closet or asks to borrow my eyeliner, it's not going to be pretty. Oh Marlboro Man, where art thou? Your comeback won't be a minute too soon!

And it appears I'm not the only one lamenting this androgynous ambiguity in male fashion. This is a growing backlash among consumers saying, "Enough already with the girly-man clothes." An article on Philly.com spoke of a new *manlier* trend in men's fashion. "'Fashion had to switch up its tactics and go from speaking to a very small segment of the male population—the metrosexual—and start speaking to the everyday Joe,' said Marshal Cohen, a chief industry analyst with market research firm NPD."[7] The article went on to define a "metrosexual" as "a man whose sense of style is sexually ambiguous. He is meticulous about grooming, from back waxes to manicures. He has excellent taste in clothing, yet he is more dandy than dapper."[8] But here's the irony: According to Cohen, fashion treated the metrosexual as "the lead dog in the race, when he was at best 11 percent of the male population."[9]

Waiting in the wings to replace the metrosexual and thus satisfy the backlash of emasculated men who are fed up with the fashion industry's attempt to pawn off the nail-buffed, latte-drinking, pink polo-wearing man as the norm, is what another article referred to as the emerging "retrosexual." "Think of him as the anti-metrosexual, the opposite of that guy who emerged in the 1990s in all his pedicured, moussed-up, skinny-jeans glory. That man-boy was searching for his inner girl, it was argued. The retrosexual, however, wants to put the *man* back into manhood."[10] Glory hallelujah. The Marlboro Man must have heard our collective cry for help.

Justin Sitron, a clinical assistant professor of education and human sexuality at Widener University states that "masculinity has been in a period of exploration in the last 20 to 25 years."[11] If we are to raise our sons to be men, we must be aware of outside influences that seek to undermine God's blueprint for our boys by redefining manhood and masculinity. Genesis 1:27 reminds us that God created man in His own image. "Male and female He created them." Men and women are different because God created them to be distinctly different. Our boys need to know it's OK to be the *man* God created them to be.

A Report Card on Boys and Academia

When it comes to boys and our current education system, something is not right. Consider that approximately 60 percent of undergraduate students enrolled in American colleges are women. Girls now outperform boys at every grade level from kindergarten through twelfth grade.[12] After college one out of three married, working women will outearn her husband. Compare this to one in ten women who outearned their husbands in the 1970s. Among workers in their twenties, 33 percent of women and only 26 percent of men have college degrees.[13]

*O*ur boys need to know it's OK to be the *man* God created them to be.

Why are boys lagging behind in school? It hasn't always been this way. R. Albert Mohler Jr., theologian and author of the book *Culture Shift*, speculates, "Many young men consider the educational environment to be frustrating, constricting, and overly feminized."[14] Decades ago there was an outcry to funnel more attention into addressing the weak links in educating girls. Special interest groups sprang forth with blueprints in place to address and cater to the learning patterns in girls in the years leading up to college, with the higher goal of increasing female enrollment in colleges and universities. New female-friendly approaches in education (for example, The Women's Educational Equity Act) were implemented to cater to the educational needs of girls and help them succeed in subjects like math and science, which had previously proven to be weak links for many girls.

Rick Johnson, author of the book *That's My Son*, notes:

The war cry of these groups in the past has been that boys were given preferential treatment in schools much to the detriment of girls. This was epitomized a dozen years ago when Wellesley College researcher Susan Bailey wrote a report that made national headlines. Titled, "How Schools Shortchange Girls," the study chronicled how teachers paid more attention to boys, steered girls away from math and science, and made schools more inviting to boys than to girls. However, a review of the facts today shows that boys are on the weak end of the educational gender gap."[15]

Take into consideration the fact that in the United States girls capture more academic honors, outscore boys in reading and writing, and score about as well on math at the fourth-, eighth-, and twelfth-grade levels on the National Assessment for Educational Progress exam.[16] "Brain research has shown differences in male and female brains that can affect preferred learning styles and communication," says Mary Ann Clark, UF associate professor of counselor education and principal investigator of an international study exploring the gender gap in education. "It has been suggested that public school curriculum may not be teaching 'to the boys' and that teaching styles are more suitable for girls."[17]

Michael Gurian, family therapist and author of *The Minds of Boys*, has trained thousands of teachers to handle the differences between girls and boys, showing them brain scans to point out the specific gender differences. And he makes suggestions on how to help boys in the classroom. "They need to touch and move things around and they need to move their bodies around and they'll learn better," he says. "The male brain many times per day just shuts down. So (boys) get bored very easily."[18] Clark agrees, stating, "The use of physical space and need for movement should be taken into consideration."[19]

Yet in spite of the finding that boys need space to move around in order to engage their brains and learn more efficiently, recess time is being drastically reduced or done away with altogether in schools across the country. Peg Tyre, author *The Trouble with Boys*, notes "In Atlanta, Georgia, and elsewhere, recess has become such a marginal part of the school day that elementary school buildings are being erected without playgrounds. Taking test scores seriously means giving up recess."[20] What a travesty! "Twenty years ago, in most public elementary schools, recess offered a daily or even twice daily respite. These days, according to the U.S. Department of Education, 39 percent of all first-graders in the country get 20 minutes a day or less of recess. Seven percent get none at all. By fourth grade, nearly half of students get less than 20 minutes a day, and 9 percent get none at all. Physical education class, which is usually required by the state, is provided one or two days a week, for less than 30 minutes."[21]

What's a Mother to Do?

As mothers of sons, God has entrusted us to nurture their hearts and encourage them to become the godly men He created them to be. Our society appears bent on waging a war against the things that grow boys into men. No wonder men today feel emasculated. At every turn they are forced to temper their testosterone and stifle their inner warrior spirit. Boys do not thrive when we treat them like girls. In the book *Wild Things*, authors (and therapists) Steven James and David Thomas say, "Instead of fighting against boys and their basic character, we must learn to work with how they were created and redirect them toward a noble vision of masculinity. Helping boys grow and mature into men means providing an environment that acknowledges and supports them in their maleness, not one that demands they be different."[22] As mothers we must be our sons' advocates and raise them in a way that celebrates manhood. Let's put a stop to this nonsense of pretending boys and girls are the same and, therefore, can be treated the same. We need to give our boys permission to be boys. If we continue to force them to comply to a sissified system of order, we will lose a generation of men.

As a society, it is to our future benefit to encourage our boys' thirst for adventure rather than neutralize it. The freedoms we have come to appreciate in our country can be traced back to a celebration of the qualities that grow boys into men. Let's face it, neutralized, androgynous men like Boy George and Michael Jackson wouldn't last a day on the front lines. For that matter, I doubt they'd last an hour in their barracks, especially if they pull out a dock-kit filled with makeup and hair products. Boys and girls are different because God created them distinctly male or female. Let's celebrate the differences rather than neutralize them under a unisex umbrella of political correctness.

> Our society appears bent on waging a war against the things that grow boys into men.

CHAPTER 2

The Wonderful World of Boys

Most every mother remembers an incident beyond the "It's a boy!" announcement that marked their sudden induction into the Boy Mama Club. For me initiation day began with special instructions from a nurse in the hospital on how to clean the navel area and ahem, you know, *"it."* When I tried to follow her instructions, I was awarded with a golden waterworks display and a chuckle from the nurse who responded to the show with, "Welcome to the wonderful world of boys!" It was almost as if my new son was sending out an advance warning: "Get ready, lady! You ain't seen nothin' yet!" And bless my heart, I hadn't. I didn't have a clue about the world of boys until I found myself smack-dab in the middle of raising my own little bundle of testosterone. And

I wouldn't trade the experience of raising my two boys for anything. In fact, they both captured my heart from day one.

Nothing compares to raising boys. Recently I was going through a box of keepsake items and stumbled upon a letter I received from my youngest son, Hayden, when he was away at camp for a week. He was nine years old at the time, and it was his first summer camp experience. He had begged to go to summer camp like his two older siblings, and finally I relented and signed the boy up. His older brother and sister had been two years older when they experienced their first summer camp, so I went back and forth after turning the paperwork in, wondering if I had made the right decision. When the time came to drop him off, I could hardly tear myself away. He looked so small next to some of the older campers! Of course, he was excited and could hardly wait for his father and me to leave. I had packed paper and self-addressed, stamped envelopes in his trunk and given him strict instructions to write home at least every other day (yes, to assuage my own worries!).

I worried myself sick during the week that followed and checked the mailbox daily hoping for a letter from him. I waited. And I waited. And I waited. Finally, toward the end of the week, I received the one and only camp letter I would ever receive from my son during all his camp years combined. Mind you, I discovered this rare camp letter from my son in the keepsake box that contained a sea of camp letters from my daughter. In her letters she provided detailed descriptions of her days and full-length bios on each new friend made. As a bonus she often added stickers or doodle drawings to jazz up her letters. Needless to say, Hayden's camp letter did not follow his sister's previously established protocol.

Following is a transcript of my much-anticipated camp letter from Hayden:

Dear parents,

We had bean burritos for lunch today and Andrew and I couldn't stop tooting so we started a tooting contest in our cabin during bunk time. I won. Camp is fun.

Love,
Hayden

That's it. No details about canoeing, horseback riding, or roasting marshmallows by a campfire. Just tooting. Which for the record, he could have done at home, for free. On the upside, at least the letter brought an end to my worry. Clearly the little lad wasn't *crying* himself to sleep each night. *Tooting* himself to sleep maybe but not crying. For the record, on pickup day, I raced toward him and was greeted with, *"Mommy, I love camp! Can I go for two weeks next summer?"* When we returned home, I opened his trunk to begin the postcamp laundry washathon, and to my absolute horror found an unused bar of soap along with five of the seven prematched and neatly folded outfits still prematched and **neatly folded**! On the upside I didn't have much wash to do.

Welcome to the world of boys where post-burrito flatulence is considered a competitive sport and hygiene, much to a mother's dismay, is optional. In this chapter we are going to discuss some factors that make our boys unique (beyond hygiene and flatulence issues). We will also discuss the unique role we, as mothers, play when it comes to communicating with our sons in order that we might set a proper foundation for the conversations to come. Somewhere at the top of our list should be an ongoing pep talk on proper hygiene, including instructions on raising the toilet seat and putting it back down. Because we all know that particular skill needs to be mastered *before* marriage.

Paving the Way for Open Communication

Author and clergyman Henry Ward Beecher once noted, "The mother's heart is the child's schoolroom." Boys view their mothers as a safe haven or a shelter from the storms of life. Whether they take a tumble off their bikes at age four or fail to make the basketball team at fourteen, mom will be there to offer encouragement and support. Author Meg Meeker, in her book *Boys Should Be Boys*, says, "When a mother extends outstretched arms to a son who has failed in sports, or school, or socially, or been deemed not smart enough, 'manly enough,' or just plain not good enough, he begins to understand what love is all about. The moment a mother extends her grace, he begins to understand that goodness in being a man isn't all about his performance. It isn't about his successes or his failures. It is about being able to accept love from another and then return that love."[1]

> *B*oys view their mothers as a safe haven or a shelter from the storms of life.

The love a boy receives from his mother will set the tone for his future relationships. I remember shortly after I met Keith, the man who would become my husband, telling my two closest girlfriends, "I think I met *him—you know, the one.*" One of their first questions was, What kind of relationship does he have with his mother? If a boy has loved and been loved by his mother, he is at an advantage when it comes to loving others. While fathers typically model acts of service to their sons and focus more on *doing*, mothers typically model acts of love and help their sons find value in *being*. If a boy is to develop into a well-rounded young man, he will need both a primary male and female influence in his life. If your son is lacking a primary male influence, set out to find positive and trusted male role models. (I will address this more in depth in conversation 5.)

In addition to modeling love to our sons, we also hold the primary position of influence when it comes to character and spiritual development. E. W. Caswell (eighteenth-century hymnwriter) said, "The mother, more than any other, affects the moral and spiritual part of the children's character. She is their constant companion and teacher in formative years. The child is ever imitating and assimilating the mother's nature. It is only in after life that men gaze backward and behold how a mother's hand and heart of love molded their young lives and shaped their destiny." Your willingness to pick up this book and read it speaks volumes about your commitment to the spiritual and character development of your son(s).

A Listening Ear

It can be difficult for boys to open up and talk about their feelings, emotions, fears, and things that matter most to them. In the book *Boys Should Be Boys*, author Meg Meeker notes, "Boys usually form stronger emotional bonds with their mothers during the early boyhood years, and it is important not to sever those bonds unnaturally or too soon. Mothers can encourage sons in areas where fathers typically don't. Being more emotionally attuned than fathers, they can see their sons' feelings and motivations more readily, and try to understand and direct them. Because many boys feel emotionally safer with their mothers, they feel less inhibited in front of them."[2]

As your son begins to pull away in his adolescent years, he may be more resistant to talk about his feelings, but that doesn't mean he doesn't have them. Look for signs of stress or indications he may need to process something that may be weighing heavy on his heart. You might offer a simple, "Hey, is everything OK? Remember, I'm here if you need to talk about anything." Resist the temptation to try to force him to open up or share more than he is comfortable sharing at the time. By simply making yourself available, it sends a message that you care and are on call to listen should he need you.

> As your son begins to pull away in his adolescent years, he may be more resistant to talk about his feelings, but that doesn't mean he doesn't have them.

As your son gets older and begins to interact more with girls, you can be a great source of wisdom to your son when it comes to unraveling the mysterious female mind. Meeker says, "A mother can teach her son about girls, because a son respects his mother even when he finds it hard to tolerate the girls at school. She teaches him to tolerate girls at various ages, to excuse their feminine behaviors that he finds ridiculous, and to appreciate that the differences between boys and girls are not good and bad, but two beneficial aspects of human nature."[3] I have had many conversations with my boys regarding the mind and motives of the average female. Let me sum them up for you:

Grade school: Son, it's true. Girls do in fact have cooties.

Middle school: Boys, steer clear. Girls your age are wicked mean. And P.S., they have cooties.

High school: Son, remember what I've told you about girls: They have cooties. And nearly half of those who are sexually active have contagious cooties called STDs and that's way worse than cooties.

I'm kidding, of course. But yeah, not really. Mothers are in a unique place to help their sons better understand girls, girl talk, and, of course, the dreaded girl drama. The irony is, I've given my sons pep talks and described the kind of girls they might want to steer clear of only to realize later, I've just described myself as a girl! It's funny how your perspective suddenly changes when you have a son who could fall prey to the kind of girl drama their own mama doled out! I recall one poor guy in the sixth grade whom I broke up with after three hours because one of my friends told me another guy (whom I had a big-time crush on) liked me. If some girl pulled that stunt on my boys, I'd be signing up for martial arts and looking up her address. Lord, please protect my boys from girls like that! Of course, for the record, justice was served because the object of my crush dumped me within twenty-four hours!

Finally, if you son confides in you or shares something that is sensitive in nature, do not share it with your friends. It takes boys a great deal of courage and trust to share their innermost thoughts and feelings, and when they do so, it's an honor and a privilege to be on the receiving end. If it gets back to your son that you shared something (even as a prayer request) he told you in confidence, he is not likely to trust you again with sensitive topics. This is especially true when it comes to their feelings about girls.

Letting Go

My house is in a neighborhood that backs up to a large greenbelt. We see deer year-round and always love the spring when we encounter a few fawn sightings. One particular spring I found a baby fawn abandoned along my backyard fence line. I could see it right out my back window and began to worry when a day had gone by and it was still alone. I feared it might not make it, so I did a little research on the Internet and discovered that it is perfectly normal for a doe to leave her young in the first week. If the mother stays close by, predators may pick up her scent and harm the fawn. Amazingly, fawns are odorless after they are born to help protect them from predators. I read further that the mothers do, in fact, return throughout the day to feed them and will even move them every so often if they feel the fawn may be in danger.

Much like a fawn's mother, a boy's mother knows when it's time to begin to pull away for the well-being of her son. In the book *Teenage Guys*, author Steve Gerali comments on this awkward dance:

> *A* boy's mother knows when it's time to begin to pull away for the well-being of her son.

As the boy begins to pull away from his mother, there is conflict between his strong need for emotional intimacy (attachment) and an equally strong need for identity (autonomy). These *attachment battles* exemplify a teenage guy's need and reluctance to connect with his mother. Mothers become aware of these attachment battles. She knows them intuitively, and she feels them acutely as they occur. This intuition or instinct is a built-in, God-designed part of mothering sons. Most mothers, unless they have some compulsive disorder, give up their sons. The greatest struggle she faces is to know when and how to let go.[4]

Is it just me or was that last sentence difficult to read? I have a lump in my throat just thinking about the struggle of *when and how to let go*. Deep in a mother's heart, she knows that when it comes time for her son to leave, he will leave both *physically* and *emotionally*. He will eventually turn his attention to another woman who will become the recipient of his adoration. Of course our sons will still love us, but their feelings won't be manifested in the same way a daughter's feelings would be toward her mother. Our role is to prepare them to love another, all the while, enjoying every minute of the brief season when we reign as queen in their hearts.

Oh Boy!

In an ironic twist of events, while writing this chapter that celebrates the uniqueness of boys, I received a call from the principal of the private high school my youngest son attends, regarding an episode of "boyish behavior." It was about nine in the morning, and he called to inform me that my son and several other junior boys showed up to school dressed in togas. Yes, togas. I assured him that I would speak to Hayden when he got home from school and make sure it didn't happen again. He was lighthearted in his tone, offering the standard cliché of "boys will be boys" before we hung up the phone. When Hayden got home from school, I asked him why he and his friends felt it would be acceptable to wear togas to school on that particular Friday morning. His answer? "Mom, it's 'relaxed dress' on Fridays, and after wearing our uniforms all week, we thought it would be fun." So there you have it. Apparently Hayden and his friends read a bit more into the term "relaxed dress" than the principal and school administrators. Yes, boys will be boys, and I for one, am proud to be a lifetime member of the Boy Mama Club.

CHAPTER 3

Wired for Adventure and a Few Trips to the Emergency Room

Recently my kids were all home for a visit, and we decided to watch old home videos. In one particular video Ryan (age five) had set a trap for his younger brother, Hayden (age eleven months) and was explaining to the video camera his "secret plan" to trick his brother into getting caught in the "trap." The "trap" was an empty cardboard appliance box sitting on its side in the corner of our living room. Leading to the entrance of the trap was about a ten-foot long trail of Cheerios (coincidentally, Hayden's snack of choice).

Ryan explained to the camera his detailed plan to entice his younger brother into the trap. On the tape I asked him, "What are you going to do if you catch your brother in the trap?" With the excitement of a kid on Christmas morning, Ryan replied, "I'm gonna close the box up, so he can't get out, and that way he won't try to get my Legos." He then motioned for me to get ready to film the big moment. Sure enough Hayden fell for the trap, crawling (and eating) his way into the cardboard prison one Cheerio at a time. Once Hayden made his way into the box, Ryan proceeded to close the flaps of the box and quickly drag a chair in front of the box to impede his brother's escape. The tape ended with Ryan doing a victory dance of some sort while Hayden's muffled cries could be heard in the background. Ah, the joys of creative play.

Chances are you could fill a book with similar accounts documenting your own son's innate sense of adventure. I doubt any mother of a son needs to be convinced that her son is wired from birth for adventure. The goal in this chapter is to help mothers find a reasonable balance when it comes to protecting their sons from danger in a way that will not stifle their God-given need for adventure. In the book *That's My Son*, author, Rick Johnson notes, "Mothers, because of their nurturing tendencies, are often overprotective of their children. After all, it's a mother's job to civilize a boy."[1] He further explains that if a boy is missing a male influence in this area, he can end up failing to learn the valuable link between taking risks and attaining success in life. This would likely explain the head-butting that commonly occurs between husbands and wives related to their sons' questionably "dangerous" adventures.

In my book *Your Boy*, I described a time when both my sons begged to pitch a tent in the backyard during the summer months. They were ages thirteen and eight at the time, and I relented at the prompting of my husband. One night turned into two nights, two nights into three, and before long my boys had practically moved their bedrooms into the tent. After one particular night of their campout adventure, they came in the following morning and excitedly shared that they had forgotten to zip up the entrance to the tent and had awakened to find a raccoon rifling through their food stash. I just about lost it; and with visions running through my mind of a raccoon showdown that resulted in trips to the ER to get a necessary series of rabies shots, I declared the campout officially over. My husband vetoed my camping ban, insisting these sorts of adventures are what separate the men from the boys. (Exactly my point, I thought. Wouldn't age eight and thirteen fall into the "boy" category?) Today I am grateful for my husband's intervention in green-lighting many of the boyhood adventures I would have otherwise squelched.

What a Mother Doesn't Know Won't Hurt Her

As mothers, one of our greatest challenges in raising our sons is finding a healthy balance when it comes to monitoring the adventures our boys may pursue. Our goal should be to protect them without stifling their innate need for adventure. In the book *Wild Things*, authors Stephen James and David Thomas note, "The male brain has more spinal fluid in the brain stem, which makes boys more physical than girls. Add to that the high level of testosterone in a boy's brain, and it's easy to see that he is programmed to be more aggressive than girls and more of a risk taker."[2]

One of our greatest challenges in raising our sons is finding a healthy balance when it comes to monitoring the adventures our boys may pursue.

John Eldridge adds, "The recipe for fun is pretty simple raising boys: Add to any activity an element of danger, stir in a little exploration, add a dash of destruction, and you've got yourself a winner."[3] During the process of writing this chapter, my oldest son, Ryan, described a recent adventure that contained every element in Eldridge's suggested recipe for fun. I had asked him to describe a memorable and "potentially dangerous" adventure he had experienced while away at college to see if there was any truth to Eldridge's theory. In return I promised him immunity for any story he shared. No scolding, no lectures. Basically a free pass. Ryan took me up on the offer and began to share about an adventure he and one of his friends had experienced. Boy, I wish I'd never asked! To this day I am haunted over the what-ifs that could have occurred in the adventure Ryan described.

To give you a bit of background, both boys are well mannered and attend church consistently on Sunday mornings. They were not a part of a fraternity or the weekend party crowd that is typical on many college campuses. Additionally, they are good students who have since graduated, one with a business degree and the other with an engineering degree. Once Ryan was thoroughly convinced of my offer of immunity, he began to share in detail about an adventure he and his buddy had had the previous semester that involved rappelling from a second-story apartment window to the ground below. I followed with the obvious question on most any mother's mind, "What in the world would possess you to do something so stupid?" His answer? Get ready because it may offer you some insight into the mysterious male mind: "Somehow it just came up, and we both admitted we'd always wanted to try it." Gulp.

With a ring of pride in his voice, Ryan went on to describe how they had stripped the bed sheets off of two twin beds in the apartment (as a side note, I doubt they had ever been washed). They then knotted the sheets together to form a make-shift rappelling rope and tied it securely to a heavy dresser. They leaned the dresser against the window, gave their rope a few test tugs, and then one at a time made their descent out the window and to the ground below. Did I mention that "the ground below" was a concrete sidewalk? You know, the kind of surface where you could bust your head wide open or, at the very least, break a leg or crack a rib should your make shift rope of bedsheets not hold up! As if the details offered weren't enough for my poor little mind to absorb, he then added, "Oh, and it was raining." Recognizing that I was nearing a point of possible hyperventilation, he went on to assure me with a matter-of-fact tone of confidence, "Mom, Winston is an engineering major. He knew what he was doing when he rigged the bed sheets to the dresser." Oh, OK. I feel so much better now. Sigh.

In the book *Boys Must Be Boys*, author Meg Meeker says, "Many teenage boys live in what psychologists refer to as 'personal fable.' This is the belief that they can do anything they want to—they have a distorted sense of their own power."[4] Apparently my son and his friend were caught up in the fable of Rapunzel, minus the damsel in distress, and of course, any brain cells. Meeker further notes, "It is extremely important for young men to learn the limits of their power. It's a challenge they feel bound to confront, and it's why they climb mountains, race cars, and wrestle. It is about understanding what they have inside and how far they can take it. It's when they hit the wall that humility begins to set in."[5]

> It is extremely important for young men to learn the limits of their power.

It will always be a mother's nature to want to rescue her son from those moments when he may hit the wall. Or in my son's case, a concrete sidewalk. Sometimes we will be successful in our attempts, while other times we may find ourselves eight hundred miles away in a happy state of ignorance is bliss. Oh, and for the record, I ignored the immunity offer and ended up giving my boy a stern lecture, complete with a never-ending list of what-ifs. As a bonus I googled the phrase: "boy fell from second story window" and then proceeded to send him several links to real-life accounts of boys who suffered from broken bones after attempting a similar stunt. In a nutshell I probably left him *wanting* to jump out a second story window! Sadly there was no shortage of stories, which lends further evidence to the fact that boys are wired for adventure. Rick Johnson notes, "Getting hurt physically, failing, persevering, and succeeding (despite overwhelming odds) are key factors in a male's growth toward manhood."[6]

You Can't Take the Nature Out of the Boy

I took up running about a year ago. Several times a week I run a two- to three-mile course on a main road that winds through my neighborhood. Along the main connector road in my neighborhood are countless coves and cul-de-sacs complete with backyard trampolines and basketball goals in every other driveway. It is suburban heaven. Yet something is missing. Rarely do I see kids out playing during my evening runs. It doesn't matter if it's summertime or after school hours during the school year, they are MIA. I do, however, run by a gated park that is typically filled with preschool aged children. Strollers line the outside entrance, and I can't help but smile when I run by. I love hearing the familiar park sounds of squeaking swings, gravel crunching under the weight of toddler feet, and gentle reprimands from mothers to "stop throwing the gravel."

As I continue my run down the main road, I am struck by the empty cul-de-sacs. Where are the grade-school kids who should be playing tag or running through their neighbor's sprinklers on a dare? Or how about the middle-school kids who should be riding their bikes to friends' houses or playing a pickup game of horse in someone's driveway? It saddens me that today's kids are missing out on outdoor play. With the increasing load of homework at every grade level and the prevalence of dual-income families and the resulting increase of kids in after-care programs, empty cul-de-sacs have become the suburban norm. Added to the list of other possible causes—the lure of video games, cable TV, and the computer—and you begin to see the problem for what it is. We've simply gotten our priorities out of order.

When I was growing up, we lived outside. During the school year we rushed to finish our homework each afternoon so we could head to the end of my street (a cul-de-sac) where neighbor kids of all ages gathered for a game of kickball or spud (a variation of dodgeball). We played nonstop until our mothers stepped out on the front porch and yelled down the street that dinner was ready. Some of us had dogs who would faithfully hang out near where we played and accompany us on the walk back home. When I walked through the door, I was an exhausted, sweaty mess. During the summertime we practically lived outdoors. In Texas the temperature can reach one hundred degrees or more, but we never seemed to notice. If we got too hot, we would duck into someone's house to cool off, have a quick snack, polish off a pitcher of Kool-Aid, and head right back out for more fun.

Boys especially suffer when outdoor play is not a common part of their day. Sadly they are missing out on the blessing of experiencing adventure in its truest form: the kind of adventure born in the great outdoors.

In *Wild at Heart* author John Eldridge notes, "In the record of our beginnings, the second chapter of Genesis makes it clear: Man was born in the outback, from the untamed part of creation. Only afterward is he brought to Eden. And ever since then boys have never been at home indoors, and men have had an insatiable longing to explore."[7]

> *Boys* especially suffer when outdoor play is not a common part of their day.

As you read that, you may be wondering why your son begs to stay indoors so he can get to the next level on his video game if he was as Eldridge says, "born for the outback." We'll talk more about the lure of video games and other things that can hinder our boys from engaging in outdoor play in conversation 2. More important, we'll discuss how we can help them choose healthier outlets for adventure. (In other words: Get off their duffs, put the game controllers down, and *go outside!*)

In the book *Boys Should Be Boys*, author Meg Meeker, M.D., says, "Some scholars say that the male brain is wired to enjoy the outdoors, starting with the fact that boys are visually more attracted to movement—including, presumably, the movement of game through the woods—than girls are. Other psychologists attribute the male fascination with nature to a desire for, a memory of, freedom—boys see nature as a larger arena where they can roam and daydream, and men feel that in the outdoors they can safely express their aggressive tendencies in sports or hunting."[8]

While working on this chapter, my oldest son, Ryan, was home for a visit. He was trading text messages with one of his best guy buddies, Dustin, and began to laugh out loud. When I asked him what was so funny, he read me the series of text messages:

Dustin: Quick question. Do you have a BB gun?

Ryan: I like where this is headed. I think we have one somewhere in the garage. Why do you ask?

Dustin: I want to hunt, shoot, and eat local birds. Can I count on you to be a Lewis to my Clark?

Ryan: I'm disappointed you felt a need to even ask.

Ryan and Dustin will have graduated from college, gotten married, and begun their new full-time jobs in the working world. Even though they are certifiable, self-supporting grown-ups, I don't see their sense of adventure waning in the least. John Eldridge notes, "Adventure, with all its requisite danger and wildness, is a deeply spiritual longing written into the soul of man. The masculine heart needs a place where nothing is prefabricated, modular, nonfat, zip lock, franchised, on-line, microwavable. Where there are no deadlines, cell phones, or committee meetings. Where there is room for the soul. Where, finally, the geography around us corresponds to the geography of our heart."[9]

I realize some of you reading this may have sons who don't actively seek out adventure and like to play it safe. Maybe they are more timid than most other boys and gravitate toward staying in an air-conditioned house rather than hiking to the creek with their friends to fish. Or maybe they have other talents that lend themselves to a more sedentary pace. Boys are wired for adventure, but not all boys will attempt to satisfy their longing for adventure in the same way. King David is a wonderful example of a well-balanced man who was a warrior fighting battles on some days and a gentle, harp-playing composer on other days. Some boys may need more of a nudge when it comes to finding their recipe for adventure. Sitting in front of a TV and getting to the next level on their favorite video game is not a true adventure and will only serve as a temporary, false substitute.

If your son is the more sedentary type, make it your mission to expose him to some of the more sedentary adventures like camping, hiking, fishing, rock collecting, canoeing, and other fresh-air activities. Organizations like the Boy Scouts or church mission trips are another way to expose our sons to a wide variety of adventures. Competitive sports can be a healthy outlet for many boys and give them a sense of teamwork and satisfaction that comes from working toward a goal. In a world full of noisy distractions that bid for their constant attention, it's important to teach our boys the value of "unplugging" from technology and spending time in the outdoors.

> *B*oys are wired for adventure, but not all boys will attempt to satisfy their longing for adventure in the same way.

A boy never outgrows his need for adventure. As mothers, we will need to develop a healthy balance when it comes to cultivating our sons' innate sense of adventure without overprotecting them in the process or, for that matter, not protecting them at all. Whether you involve your son in competitive team sports, hunting, fishing, camping, hiking, scouting, or any other number of outdoor activities, what matters most is that you get him outside and get him outside often. The best adventures for boys occur in the open outdoors. They happen while lying zipped in sleeping bags under a canopy of twinkling stars. They happen at summer camp while roasting marshmallows by a campfire and the cologne of choice is bug repellent. They happen on dusty, Little League fields when the championship trophy is at stake and your son is playing his best friend's team. They happen on dirt piles where sword fights with sticks will determine the reigning king of the hill. They happen on fishing trips taken with Dad where they will eat their catch and come home smelling like campers. They happen in neighborhood cul-de-sacs with a pickup game of basketball or a game of flashlight tag after the sun goes down. And yes, they even happen in backyard tents where potentially rabid raccoons sneak in for a midnight snack . . . all while your sons sleep soundly a few feet away.

CHAPTER 4

Warning: Helicopter Moms Are Dangerous to a Boy's Health

everal years ago I posted a vintage home movie clip on my blog of my boys (ages four and nine at the time) sledding down our carpeted stairs on a giant piece of cardboard. Similar to the baby who is more interested in playing with the box on Christmas morning than the shiny toy inside the box, the point of the post was to support the theory that some of the best forms of creative play are not found on the aisles of toy stores but, rather, right under our noses. After I posted the vintage clip, many moms commented that they too had plenty of pictures and video footage of their kids engaged in good, clean, (and *free!*) fun to back up the theory.

That is, except for *one* mom of who took me to the virtual woodshed. She mentioned that she, too, has sons and then proceeded to let me have it for: (1) allowing my sons to engage in such "a dangerous activity" and (2) being irresponsible for posting the clip and, therefore, "encouraging other mothers to allow their children to engage in dangerous activities." When I read her comment, I just shook my head back and forth and mumbled a "bless her heart," before clicking delete. Actually, *bless her boys' hearts!* It's time for this mama to bring her inner helicopter in for a landing before she ends up with a couple of thirty-year-old mama's boys. She would surely have a panic attack if I post the story on my blog about my college son and his friend rappelling from the second-story window of their friend's apartment using bedsheets as a makeshift rope. I'm fairly certain the last chapter would have put her over the edge and left her wanting to organize a good old fashioned book burning. But only in a controlled burning area with appropriate flame-retardant clothing and a certified fire marshal present.

One of the greatest threats to a boy's budding manhood and quest for adventure is the ever-present and overprotective "helicopter mom." Like the poor mother who chastised me for allowing my boys to sled down carpeted stairs, a growing legion of these hovering mothers have lined up to drink the Kool-Aid when it comes to overparenting. Some have bubble-wrapped their children from a world of potential dangers while others micromanaged their children's lives down to the tiniest detail. Innocently, many of these mothers rationalize that they are investing in the future livelihood of their children, yet in reality many of their children will lack the necessary survival skills to make it in the real world.

Consider the following list of hovering behaviors to see whether you qualify as a helicopter mom.

You might be a "helicopter mom" if you:

- Repeatedly deliver your son's lunch/backpack/gym clothes/ etc. to the school when he leaves it behind.
- Are hesitant to take the training wheels off your son's bike and he is entering middle school.
- Help manage your middle/high-schooler's Day-timer and keep track of his assignment/test due dates. (Bonus points if you know his last three test grades.)
- Require your son to carry hand sanitizer and lather up before/after every meal/snack and bathe in it after playing outside.
- Require your son to wear flame-retardant sleepwear to bed after age ten, as opposed to other logical alternatives: (1) The outfit he wore that day or (2) his skivvies.
- Actually followed the recommended protocol of sterilizing pacifiers/toys/bottle nipples. (Exception: You get a free pass if he was your first child; after that you're guilty.)
- Find yourself saying things like: "We're registered to take the SAT this Saturday" or "We're going to play coach-pitch baseball next year instead of tee-ball," (Key word: "we're").
- Have stayed up working on a class project/paper/etc. after your son has gone to bed so he can turn it in on time and not face a late penalty.
- Have signed your son up for more than two extracurricular activities in one season. (And even two can be excessive, depending on the type of activity and time required.)
- Have contacted your son's teacher/coach to argue an injustice (such as not enough playing time in the game or a failure to make the A team rather than require your son to address the problem on his own).

Truth be told, most moms, myself included, are guilty at some level of lapsing into helicopter-mom mode on occasion. It's a mother's nature to protect our children from the dangers of the world and look for ways to help them get ahead. However, we actually do our sons more harm and we "provoke them to wrath" when we are overprotective (Col. 3:21). As parents, the key is to find a healthy balance by being "protectors" without becoming "provokers."

Please note that I am not advocating irresponsible parenting where kids are allowed to ride their bikes without helmets, eat endless amounts of junk food for dinner, and roam the streets on the weekends with no curfew. Helicopter moms behave in a manner that is extreme in nature. They can stifle a boy's pursuit of adventure by labeling his adventurous spirit as a bad thing when, in fact, God intended it to be a good. A boy's sense of adventure is a necessary stepping-stone along the journey to manhood.

The key is to find a healthy balance by being "protectors" without becoming "provokers."

Consider this excerpt from an article in *Time* magazine addressing the overparenting trend (and a growing backlash):

Overparenting had been around long before Douglas MacArthur's mom Pinky moved with him to West Point in 1899 and took an apartment near the campus, supposedly so she could watch him with a telescope to be sure he was studying. But in the 1990s something dramatic happened, and the needle went way past the red line. From peace and prosperity, there arose fear and anxiety; crime went down, yet parents stopped letting kids out of their sight;

the percentage of kids walking or biking to school dropped from 41% in 1969 to 13% in 2001. Death by injury has dropped more than 50% since 1980, yet parents lobbied to take the jungle gyms out of playgrounds, and strollers suddenly needed the warning label "Remove Child Before Folding." Among 6-to-8-year-olds, free playtime dropped 25% from 1981 to '97, and homework more than doubled. Bookstores offered *Brain Foods for Kids: Over 100 Recipes to Boost Your Child's Intelligence.* The state of Georgia sent every newborn home with the CD *Build Your Baby's Brain Through the Power of Music,* after researchers claimed to have discovered that listening to Mozart could temporarily help raise IQ scores by as many as 9 points. By the time the frenzy had reached its peak, colleges were installing Hi, Mom! Web cams in common areas, and employers like Ernst & Young were creating "parent packs" for recruits to give Mom and Dad, since they were involved in negotiating salary and benefits.[1]

Patricia Somers of the University of Texas at Austin spent more than a year studying the species of helicopter parents and found there are even helicopter grandparents, who turn up with their elementary-school grandchildren for college-information sessions aimed at juniors and seniors.[2]

And speaking of college, I sat in a parent/student meeting at a college orientation for incoming freshmen where an academic advisor issued a gentle yet clear warning to parents: Don't call us, we'll call you (but, probably not, so don't wait by the phone). Ouch! She then went on to share a list of common overparenting abuses during the school year that include the ever popular, "I want to check on my child's grades." Or, "How does my child go about changing majors?" There's even the ever-increasing, "My child's roommate is not a good match and we need to request a midsemester change." Excuse me, "we"? Is mama bear sleeping on a trundle in the same room, or something?

If we were to examine a root cause of hovering, it would most likely be grounded in a need to be in control. Some mothers have a tendency to overprotect their children because they are seeking control over dangers (both real and perceived) that threaten to harm their children. Other mothers may obsess over their children's homework assignments, school schedules, and overall academic progress in order to control their destiny and, thus, provide them with future happiness. They incorrectly believe the formula: good grades = good colleges = success in the real world = happily ever after. Yet other mothers may hover when it comes to image-maintenance issues such as staying in shape, dressing attractively (or wearing name brands), having the latest gadgets, or even driving a cool car.

While at first glance, hovering helicopter moms may appear to have their child's best interests in mind, their high need for control can be classified as a form of fear-based parenting. Fear of danger. Fear their child will not find future success (a relative term). And fear their child may not be accepted among his peers if he doesn't look/perform a certain way. In a nutshell, helicopter moms, like most all moms, worry they will be to blame if their children don't "turn out" or aren't accepted.

For those of you who are carrying mounds of guilt over such things as a failure to go over your youngest child's math drill cards (guilty as charged!) or a failure to spend as much time reading to the youngest child (guilty as charged, again!) or even failing to know which math course your youngest child is currently enrolled in (guilty yet again!), let me encourage you with this little bit of irony: My youngest scored a perfect eight hundred on the math portion of the SAT and was the only one of our children to earn an academic scholarship to college. Go figure. By default of the fact he is the youngest child, I was too tired to hover over him regarding grades, activities, resume boosters, and other forms of guaranteeing success like I did with his older siblings. If I had known then what I now know, I would have clocked out sooner and traded my helicopter for a cruise ship bound for the Caribbean.

In fact, the *Time* article I mentioned previously addresses this paradox by giving us all a little food for thought when it comes to the tendency to overparent: "We can fuss and fret and shuttle and shelter, but in the end, what we do may not matter as much as we think."[3] The article cites a finding by the authors of the popular book *Freakonomics* who analyzed a Department of Education study tracking the progress of kids through fifth grade. They found that variables such as how much parents read to their kids and how much TV kids watch, among other variables, ultimately make little difference. In an interview with *USA Today*, the authors concluded, "Frequent museum visits would seem to be no more productive than trips to the grocery store."[4] This is certainly food for thought for those of us who have put in overtime hours when it comes to managing our children's lives in an effort to protect them and help them "get ahead" in the world. It looks like those expensive Baby Einstein toys and Hooked on Phonics tapes may not get them into Harvard after all. But letting them sled down the stairs on the cardboard packaging they came in just might do the trick.

My husband and I are both firstborn children who were involved in competitive sports and thoroughly enjoy watching our children compete in their chosen sports. As I've matured in the faith over the years, I've learned to rein myself in when I begin to place an unhealthy emphasis on my own sons' sports endeavors. My youngest son is a good all around athlete who excels in just about every sport he plays. After wrapping up a season of football in his junior year, he was days shy of trying out for his school's varsity basketball team. He's an outstanding basketball player, and the varsity coach had even pulled him aside and encouraged him to try out for the team. My husband and I were looking forward to watching him play another season of basketball when suddenly he announced on the week of tryouts that he wanted to play in a city recreational league. Instead of playing for the varsity team, he would instead be playing for a team called the Boss Hoggz along with some of his friends.

Of course, the rec league is not nearly as competitive as the school league, so my husband and I were stunned when our son approached us and announced he wanted to join the Boss Hoggz. Had it been our first child (who by default of being the firstborn child of two firstborn parents will probably need some counseling to reverse the damage of stealth-helicopter parenting), we likely would have put our foot down and made him play for the school team. With our younger son, we reined in our own desires and reasoned (1) He already plays football and runs track for the school. (2) He's entitled to a little fun. (3) It would give him extra time to focus on spiritual things like attending the Wednesday evening youth group Bible study. And (4) in the scheme of all eternity, what does it really matter?

One of Hayden's greatest high school memories will be playing for the Boss Hoggz. These guys had so much fun. They had T-shirts and backpacks made with the team logo and wore them proudly to school. Sometimes there were more fans at their games than at their school's varsity basketball games! They showed up dressed in their required jersey but partnered it with obnoxious shorts and black crew socks. During the games they hooted and hollered for one another and even turned cartwheels when a teammate scored. Keith and I absolutely loved every minute of watching these guys play, but most important we loved seeing our son thoroughly enjoy himself in the process. And to top it off, they won first place in their recreation league!

Helicopter Mom to the Rescue!

In order to develop a healthy masculinity, boys will attempt to break away from their mothers at various stages in the growing-up journey. This is a natural occurrence that if stifled can inhibit their quest to become men. Moms who hold tightly to their boys or, worse yet, come to their rescue every time they face consequences from mistakes or irresponsible actions will breed a sense of prolonged dependency in their sons. And if there was ever a mom to come to the rescue, it's the helicopter mom. You've seen her before. She's the one zipping into a parking lot at the school, jogging into the school with a leap and bound as she delivers little Johnny's lunch to the office. Again. For the third time this month. With a sweet note written on little Johnny's napkin because that's what helicopter moms do. They rescue their sons from negative consequences because negative consequences are unpleasant.

> *In order to develop a healthy masculinity, boys will attempt to break away from their mothers at various stages in the growing-up journey.*

The *Time* article I cited previously described one elementary school principal in Kansas who got so fed up with parents rescuing their children, she established a "no rescue" policy. Her breaking point came when she noticed the front-office table covered day after day with forgotten lunch boxes and notebooks, all brought in by parents. Gulp. Guilty as charged. I pulled the mom-to-the-rescue stunt more times than I'm ashamed to admit. My breakthrough finally came on my third trip in one week to the local middle school. This time I was delivering an assignment my son left behind when all of a sudden I realized there was greater value in allowing him to suffer the consequences rather than rescue him yet again and reinforce the pattern of irresponsibility.

In the book *That's My Son,* author Rick Johnson warns,

> By running too quickly to rescue their sons when things get tough, some moms are teaching their boys that the way out of hard times is to find someone to get them off the hook rather than to be accountable to the one in authority and step up to the plate. This can set patterns for boys' entire lives. A boy who avoids accountability becomes a man who is answerable to no one—a recipe for disaster.[5]

When we rescue our sons from the consequences of their irresponsible actions and mistakes, we actually hinder their progress in the journey to manhood. Let me put it to you in a more sobering fashion: When we rescue our sons from consequences, we hinder them from becoming men and encourage them to behave like little mama's boys indefinitely. Part of becoming a man is learning to accept responsibility for irresponsible actions and mistakes, learn from the experiences, and correct the behaviors before they become a habit or pattern.

I am not suggesting we have a zero-tolerance policy for mistakes and run our homes like a military boot camp. Everyone makes mistakes, and we've all been in need of a rescue from time to time.

I recall an assignment my son failed to bring to school in his junior year of high school. His cumulative GPA was right on the borderline of what he needed in order to qualify for college academic scholarships. A simple ten-point grade deduction on a late assignment can in turn serve as a punishment of sorts to my husband and me if it means missed opportunities in the way of scholarships. I made an exception but charged my son for my time and the expense of gas. In addition, I put him to work doing the dishes when he came home so he didn't escape without consequences.

When we rescue our sons from the consequences of their irresponsible actions and mistakes, we actually hinder their progress in the journey to manhood.

If we are to help our sons become men, we must be willing to employ some tough-love parenting tactics along the way. We do them no favors when we rush to their rescue time and time again and allow them to escape without consequences. Mothers who establish this pattern will be rescuing their boys for many years to come. A friend of mine recently told me about a mother from her church who sent out a churchwide e-mail soliciting employment for her grown son, who was in his thirties. My friend was appalled, as well she should be. Further, the mother attached her son's resume and gave her e-mail address as the contact, stating she would pass along any job leads to him since he *lived at home*.

This lady isn't a mother; she's an unpaid personal assistant! It's time for mama to cut the apron strings and let her adult-aged son grow up and become a real man. This clearly isn't the first time this mom has come to her son's rescue. It probably began with a lunch that was left behind, followed by the gym clothes, a few school projects, another lunch or two, and the list goes on and on. Resist the urge to rescue your son from unpleasant consequences. If you don't, you just may find yourself working as a full-time, unpaid assistant for decades to come while your son faithfully puts in overtime on your living room sofa with a game controller in hand. Energy drinks and buffalo wings included. On your dime.

> *If* we are to help our sons become men, we must be willing to employ some tough-love parenting tactics along the way.

Dad:2:Dad

Go to VickiCourtney.com and click on the link to the 5 Conversations blog for my husband's list of activities and the books/training materials he has used with our sons to reinforce this conversation. While you're there, feel free to add your husband's ideas to the list!

What you don't learn

to conquer may become

your master.

CHAPTER 5

Raising a Wise Guy

*L*et's do a little word association game. When I say a
name, what is the first descriptive phrase that pops into
your mind? Here we go: Golf legend Tiger Woods? Former megachurch pastor Ted Haggard? Former governor of South
Carolina, Mark Sanford? Former governor of New York, Elliot
Spitzer? Or how about, Hollywood actor and producer of *Passion of
the Christ*, Mel Gibson?

I plugged each of the above names into the Google search
engine. When I did so, it automatically generated a drop-down
menu containing the most searched phrases associated with the
name. Here are the most common phrases that came up alongside
each individual name:

- **Tiger Woods:** mistress, affair, sex addict, scandal
- **Ted Haggard:** arrested, male escort, scandal, homosexual, healed
- **Mark Sanford:** mistress, affair, divorce, scandal
- **Elliot Spitzer:** call girl, scandal, mistress, prostitute
- **Mel Gibson:** rant, scandal, racist

While each of these men has had noteworthy accomplishments during the course of his life, sadly each one is now defined by his public downfall. Their past achievements have been overshadowed and replaced by tainted reputations. Some of you might be wondering, *What does this have to do with my son?* The truth is, what happened to these men can happen to any one of our sons. The scandals associated with the above-mentioned men are not the ultimate blame for their downfalls. Oh sure, the scandals triggered their *public downfalls*, but the *real downfalls* for these men began long ago, somewhere in the deep recesses of their hearts and minds.

Somewhere along the way each of these men faced a temptation and ultimately succumbed to it. Not one time or two times, but over and over again. What began as a hesitation when standing at the crossroad of temptation became second nature. Ultimately their repetition of sin bred a habit. I'm sure each one of them knew that what they were doing was wrong on some basic level, but like a drug addict in search of the next buzz, they chose to risk it all. In the end they would lose most everything. Their actions would cause untold amounts of damage to themselves, their family members, and their reputations. It would change the course of their lives forever. I bet if they could go back to the point of origin when they first stood at the crossroads of temptation, they'd slam on the brakes and rethink their decision. What they didn't conquer at the crossroads, in the end, became their master.

You don't have to be a pro athlete, politician, or charismatic church leader to suffer a downfall. Chances are, we can all think of examples of men (and women) who have been mastered by sins that, in turn, left their lives and relationships in shambles. I have a close family member who was mastered by an addiction to alcohol that nearly cost him his wife, child, and job. As it is, he lost two decades of happiness . . . all for the contents of a vodka bottle. Another couple I know has suffered the heartache of a son so addicted to heroin that he stole from them to buy drugs, was in and out of jail, and even lived on the streets for a time. Every time the doorbell or phone rang they wondered if it would be someone to notify them of their son's death. I have numerous friends who have been blind-sided by the discovery of their husbands' affairs. Some of the marriages survived and some did not. I have another friend who received a call in the middle of the night from her Sunday-school-teaching husband who was away on business. He had been arrested for soliciting a prostitute and was forced to call her so she could find him legal representation. Her world was shattered in a matter of moments. Facing criminal charges and a court date, he had no choice but to come clean with his wife about his double life. Sadly I've had far too many friends who have experienced the secondhand fallout from husbands or sons who are mastered by an addiction to porn.

You don't have to be a pro athlete, politician, or charismatic church leader to suffer a downfall.

Enslavement to sin always produces collateral damage. Just ask Tammy, who answered a survey question I posted on my blog where I asked mothers to share their main concerns when it comes to raising sons. She says, "My husband of fifteen years, with a nine-year old daughter and a six year-old son, one day decided he was going to abandon his family and marry another woman thirteen years younger than me. Within nine months of his leaving, he had his vasectomy reversed and was remarried. In their first year of marriage he had another child, a boy. He has had little to no interaction with our children since, in over four years. My question/concern is: How do I teach my son to be morally sound when he has been exposed to such blatant infidelity?"

I realize that many of you are like Tammy, going it alone when it comes to raising your sons to be godly men. Please don't be discouraged or give up hope. Your efforts will make a difference. Enslavement to sin always produces collateral damage. By exposing your son to God's truths, the hope is that he will ultimately recognize that true freedom can only be found in Christ.

Enslavement to sin always produces collateral damage.

A downfall doesn't officially become a downfall when someone leaves their spouse, is caught looking at porn, or arrested for embezzlement. A downfall begins at the point of enslavement. In fact, many who are experiencing a downfall will never be caught or discovered. The reason I've devoted an entire conversation to the dangers of enslavement is that many of these men, if given the challenge to trace their downfall back to the point of origin (the original stand-at-the-crossroads moment of truth), would likely find themselves back in their middle, high school, or college years. While we can't control the choices our sons will make when standing at a tempting crossroad, we can educate them about the fallout that can result from being mastered by sin.

In this chapter we will address several external factors that if practiced, can help protect our sons from enslavement to certain sins. In the next chapter we will look at the topic of mastery from more of an internal perspective. More important, I will give you an easy-to-remember formula to pass along to your sons that will help them practice self-control when faced with a tempting situation. Chapter 7 will deal specifically with the topic of pornography. Sadly many boys are exposed to porn at a young age, which puts them at greater risk of being mastered by it. Therefore I felt it necessary to devote an entire chapter to the topic of porn, and more important, steps we can take to equip our sons to make wise and godly choices when they are exposed to the temptation.

Finally, if you have younger sons and are perhaps wondering if this conversation is relevant to your current season of parenting, let me encourage you to keep reading. You may have heard the saying, "The best time to plant a tree was ten years ago. The second best time is now." Much of what we are going to discuss is most effective if introduced and implemented in the early years. In other words, you are getting a jump-start on the problem. The minute your son displays an impulsive desire to pursue something that is not good for him is the moment he is ready to learn some basic and godly principles of self-control. In addition, it's an added benefit if the information we will discuss in this conversation is on your radar before your son is engaged in the battle. In a sense you will be in a position to train your son on how to use some powerful weapons before the battle ever begins. Not to mention, I'm a big fan of taking preventative measures on the front end versus reacting to the fallout on the back end.

As moms, we have essentially two lines of defense when it comes to training our sons to make wise and godly choices (in addition to prayer, of course):

1. Address the *external factors* that can better equip our sons to make godly choices (the topic of this chapter).
2. Address the *internal factors* that can better equip our sons to make godly choices (the topic of the next chapter).

As we look at external factors that can better equip our sons to make godly choices, I want to focus on three primary factors: The parent factor, the friend factor, and the God factor. As the mother of two now grown (at least out-of-the-nest) sons, I can speak firsthand to the benefits of each factor when it comes to building a foundation of godly character in their lives. When all three factors are implemented together in unison, the likelihood they will be mastered by sin is greatly reduced.

The Parent Factor

Caring, engaged parents typically raise happier and healthier children. In fact, the following findings were detailed in an article published on USAToday.com entitled, "Teens Do Better with Parents Who Set Limits."[1]

- Teens who had a bedtime of 10:00 p.m. or earlier, set by parents, got more sleep and were less likely to be depressed or consider suicide than those allowed to stay up past midnight.
- Teen drivers whose parents set and enforced rules were more likely to wear seat belts and less likely to speed,

get in crashes, drink and drive, or use cell phones while driving.

- Teens whose parents set rules also smoke less, delay sex, and do better in school.

Parenting is hard work and takes tremendous amounts of time and energy. It takes time to teach and train a child. It takes time to draw up boundaries; it takes time to maintain the boundaries; and it takes time to enforce the boundaries when they are crossed.

Even if you are an engaged and attentive parent, you still must contend with parents of your child's friends who are not. A couple of years ago my youngest son was attending a new high school after being in private school for the preceding years. He went from an environment where we knew his friends and his friends' parents to an environment where we knew little (if anything) about his new friends. He has always made friends easily and within a few weeks was invited to watch a college football game "with a bunch of kids" over at a new friend's house (guys and girls). After the game the guys were invited to spend the night. Being an engaged parent, I called in advance to thank the parents for hosting the party and basically to make sure they were going to be there the entire time to supervise the event. Unfortunately my call was not appreciated. I began by thanking the dad for the invitation my son received and then followed with, "I just wanted to make sure you were going to be there to supervise since it sounds like most of the ninth-grade class will be there." At that moment his tone changed, and he became abrupt and rude. "Well, I can't promise you we're going to stick around the entire time, but my oldest son will be there and he's in college." Nice. He was even kind enough to offer me a bit of parenting wisdom before hanging up. "You know, you can't watch your kids 24–7. You have to let kids be kids." Sorry Pops, but if letting "kids be kids" means leaving a few dozen ninth-grade girls and guys alone in your house to engage in standard ninth-grade kid like behaviors, I'll pass on the invitation to the party. Perhaps the most disturbing part of the call was at the end when he admitted my call had caught him off guard because he had never received a call from a parent "checking things out" before a gathering.

The truth is, we can't protect our sons twenty-four hours a day from making foolish choices, but we *can* set up boundaries and rules to make it more difficult for them to make foolish choices. And we can certainly limit their exposure to situations where other parents are contributing to the pursuit of foolishness by failing to supervise the children in their care. There is great value in helping your son find friends who have like-minded parents. This doesn't mean you should forbid your son from hanging out with kids who don't have engaged and caring parents, but you need to find a protective balance.

Even if you are an engaged and attentive parent, you still must contend with parents of your child's friends who are not.

The Friend Factor

> He who walks with wise men will be wise, but the
> companion of fools will suffer harm. (Prov. 13:20 NASB)

Several months ago a friend of mine was completely caught off guard when she discovered that her good, Christian daughter had been sneaking off to smoke pot with her group of friends. She made the comment, "I just don't understand how this could happen. Every day I pray God will protect my children and help them make wise choices." My friend is a good mother and a faithful prayer warrior, but she failed to address some obvious external factors that she had dismissed as unimportant, like for example, paying a bit more attention to her daughter's peer group and limiting her daughter's contact with some of the kids who had well-known reputations for being partiers.

The type of friends your son chooses or gravitates toward can speak volumes about his developing identity. It's hard to say whether "identity determines peer group" or "peer group determines identity," but the point is really moot. Either way, when your son conforms to a peer group, it can have a positive or negative outcome on his behavior.

Benjamin Franklin once said, "He who lies down with the dogs shall rise up with fleas." If you've ever had to treat a flea-infested dog, I think you would agree that it's far better to take preventive measures on the front end than tackle the problem after the fact.

When it comes to choosing a positive peer group, one distinction we have made in our home is the difference between *weekday friends* and *weekend friends.* A weekday friend might be someone my son meets at school or an after-school activity. The friendship is primarily built during school hours or during the time spent in a common activity. Any time spent after school or on weekends would be at our home in a monitored environment. A weekend friend might be someone who has similar beliefs and values as my son. I would not hesitate to have this child over on the weekends or allow my son to spend time with the friend away from our house. Obviously, the weekend friend list is a much shorter list than the weekday friend list.

Having taught our children this distinction, we had a baseline for helping them choose a positive peer group that is parent-approved. For example, if my son expressed a desire to get together with a weekday friend from school, and it was a friend we didn't know, we had the condition that the friend come to our house until we can get a better gauge on the situation. The friend may or may not transition into a weekend friend. In some situations our sons had friends they strictly saw at our home because we did not have an adequate comfort level in allowing our sons to spend time at the friend's house, like for example, the situation I mentioned earlier where my son received the invitation to a party that was going to be essentially unsupervised.

In a study conducted by The National Longitudinal Study of Adolescent Health, researchers concluded that parents have a good reason to get to know their children's friends, as well as the parents of their children's friends. Based on their findings, here are some ways researchers suggested parents can remain vigilant about the influence of their child's peer group:[2]

- Look beyond your child's best friend to his or her close circle and wider peer group to understand the full range of peer influence.
- Pay attention to the composition of your teen's immediate circle of friends.
- Focus more on your teen's positive friends. These are the peers who are making a difference. Helping young people sustain positive relationships with good role models is protective.
- Learn about the relationships your child's friends have with their parents. By steering your children to friends who are close to their own parents, you can help reduce risk.

Let me also add that it may be necessary in some cases to completely ban your son from high-risk associations for a season (or sometimes permanently) when boundary lines are crossed or trust is breached. Both of my sons experienced a major stand-at-the-crossroads, life-defining situation in their high school years. Keith and I have always prayed that if (when) our sons stray from the path of God, they will be caught in their sin as early as possible. Simply put, we asked God to sound the sin alarm to "Repent! Turn back!" Should our children respond by hitting the snooze button, we wanted them caught, so we could intervene in an effort to (1) address the problem at its root cause and (2) protect them from straying any farther down the path before they develop a negative habit or pattern. In a nutshell, we wanted them caught before they could hit the snooze button.

In the situations where my sons were caught engaging in a sinful activity, they were immediately placed on lockdown. In addition to seizing their cell phones, laptops, and car keys (with the exception of driving to school and work), we also banned them from associating with anyone else who had been involved in the situation until we could get a better grasp on the situation. We reasoned that these "friends" were not a good influence on our sons, and our sons were in turn not a good influence on their friends.

Because a breach of trust had occurred, the burden of responsibility was placed on each of our sons to earn our trust back before privileges were reinstated. In the situations we identified certain boys who, because of a proven track record of distrust and a lack of repentance, were put on the banned friend list permanently unless they could prove otherwise. The first psalm reminds us, "My son, if sinners entice you, do not give in to them . . . do not go along with them, do not set foot on their paths; for their feet rush into sin

(Ps. 1:10, 15–16). Until our sons have the wisdom and discernment to keep a distance from those who might "entice" them or tempt them to "rush into sin," it's up to us to help them keep a distance. I know this sounds harsh but, given the power of peer influence, we have a responsibility to protect our sons, and sometimes this means drawing boundaries that would aid in protecting them from *themselves*.

The friend ban forced both of my sons to seek out new friends or make an effort to reconnect with old friends who were at least making an effort to follow Christ. In the end God provided each of our sons with a handful of solid Christian friends. Today our sons view the "friend intervention" as a much needed wake-up call that in the end helped nudge them back to God's path.

We have been fortunate that for the most part our sons have made overall good choices when it comes to their immediate peer group. The few bumps we experienced along the way served as tangible reminders of God's wisdom when it comes to choosing friends. Truly, "bad company corrupts good character" (1 Cor. 15:33). In spite of our time and attention invested in teaching them this truth, sometimes our sons will simply have to learn the hard way. In the meantime we can do our part by keeping tabs on their peer group and steering them to friends who share the same values and beliefs.

How Well Do You Know Your Child's Peers?[3]

1. Name your child's best friend.
2. Name your child's next closest five or six friends.
3. Do you know those friends' ages?
4. Name those friends' parents' first names.
5. Describe those friends' relationships with their parents.
6. Name as many young people as you can in your child's peer group (usually about fifty individuals).
7. Describe the social and behavioral characteristics of the leading (most popular) crowd at your child's school.
8. Describe the social and behavioral characteristics of your child's school.

The God Factor

In the book *Boys Should Be Boys*, author and pediatrician Meg Meeker says, "I say this not as a theologian myself, but as pediatrician, and base it on what I have seen in my clinical practice. Boys who adhere to a traditional religious practice are far more likely to be able to withstand the pressures of life, to have a sense of wholeness and purpose about themselves, than boys who have either been raised with no faith or with a formless self-directed faith."[4]

As I was writing this chapter, my younger son was preparing to attend a high school prom with some of his longtime friends from the church youth group. Looking at their pictures, I was overwhelmed with gratitude for the provision of this group of friends. They have grown up in the church together, having experienced everything from preschool to VBS to youth group camps and events. They've done Wednesday night Bible studies together and traveled on weeklong mission trips. In fact, the four boys represented in the picture began their friendship as port-a-crib neighbors in the church nursery. They did father-son campouts and attended one another's birthday parties over the years. A couple months prior to the prom, they spent their spring break vacation on a mission trip to Thailand.

They are a great group of kids. Not perfect, mind you, but who is? Some of them (just like us) have hit bumps along the way in their high school years that knocked them off course for a season. If you asked them about those bumps in the road, they'd tell you it helped define not only *who* they are today but also *where* they are in their Christian journey. In fact, I have witnessed a neat dynamic take place with this group of kids over the past few years. If one of them strayed a bit from God's path, the others seemed to take notice and lovingly encourage their friend back into the fold. My own son has been the encourager at times, as well as the one on the receiving end of the encouragement.

> *If* one of them strayed a bit from God's path, the others seemed to take notice and lovingly encourage their friend back into the fold.

One of the reasons this group wanted to attend the prom together was because they had no interest in engaging in standard prom activities like drinking, grinding, and an overnight stay in a hotel room with their dates. They just wanted to have fun—good, clean, wholesome fun—the kind of fun they'll remember for many years to come. Seeing the pictures of this amazing group of kids reminds me that it is possible to raise kids who are counter culture. Again, that doesn't mean they won't have slipups along the way.

They are up against the same temptations as anyone else, but they have a built-in network of support in their faith.

If I had to come up with the common denominators that differentiate the group of kids who attended prom together from many other students their same age, it would be the following: (1) they were raised by committed Christian parents in the Christian faith from a young age; (2) their parents are faithful church attenders who are committed to being involved in their local church (vs. sporadic Sunday attenders); and (3) their parents were diligent in guiding them to choose friends with a like-minded set of beliefs and values. Amazingly each of the common denominators above represents the external factors we have addressed in this chapter: the parent factor, the friend factor, and the God factor. But most important, each one is dependant on parent implementation. The first step to protecting our sons from being mastered by temptation and sin is to expose them to an environment that provides them with the one and only solution: a close and thriving relationship with Jesus Christ.

CHAPTER 6

The Secret to Self-Control

It is better to be patient than powerful; it is better to have
self-control than to conquer a city. (Prov. 16:32)

In the summer prior to my older son's sophomore year in high school, he learned a valuable life lesson that won't soon be forgotten. He and a good friend had been waiting with much anticipation for a new video game to release. When it released just days into the summer, they were first in line to get the game. In the week that followed, they holed themselves up in my home office in front of the computer in a frenzied attempt to get to the next level in the game. One week turned to two, two weeks to four, and before you knew it, the summer was gone.

While I sometimes stepped in and made them take a break and go outside, it was as if they had a one-track mind and could think of nothing more than getting to the next level of that ridiculous video game. I held back on the urge to ban playing it altogether, hoping he would eventually come to the conclusion that it was nothing more than a time waster. Sure enough my plan worked. By the end of the summer, my son grew weary of playing the game only to realize the summer was now gone. I remember him saying something to the effect of "I can't believe I wasted my whole summer playing that stupid game." Of course, his siblings were all too happy to rub it in with taunts of being a "gaming nerd" who will never be able to get a girlfriend or for that matter a job.

My son is now out of college, married, and a responsible member of the working community. To this day he speaks of that summer before his sophomore year and the deep regret he and his friend felt when they realized they traded a whole summer for a silly game. However, the summer wasn't entirely wasted. My son learned a few valuable lessons in the process. He was faced with a temptation that threatened to master him and all but did for a summer. My son and his friend were captives to a game that promised nothing more than a series of short temporary thrills, the reward of getting to the next level. How ironic that a game they forfeited their entire summer to master, in the end, mastered them.

Our boys would be wise to learn from Paul's counsel: "Everything is permissible for me—but not everything is beneficial. Everything is permissible for me—but I will not be mastered by anything" (1 Cor. 6:12). If our sons don't learn the godly attribute of self-control, they will be at risk of becoming "a slave to whatever has mastered them" (2 Pet. 2:19). Porn, alcohol, drugs, sex, dating relationships, video games, and other common boyhood temptations will cross their paths at some point on the journey to manhood. Sure, we need to draw reasonable boundaries in an effort to protect them (oftentimes, from themselves), but we won't always be there to guide them to make good and godly choices. We don't want to raise sons who simply behave as the result of snazzy behavior-modification tactics gleaned from the latest and greatest parenting book (whether mine or any other). Self-control is one of the fruits of the Spirit mentioned in Galatians 5:22–23 and is arguably a godly discipline that is mastered only by the indwelling of the Holy Spirit. However, parents can do certain things to introduce basic principles of self-control into their sons' lives at a young age, long before they may surrender their hearts to Christ.

In an effort to introduce the concept of self-control to even the youngest boys, I came up with a fairly simple formula that is easy to remember and provides a foundation to build on over the years: "Stop, think, pray" or for short, STP. (If they can remember "stop, drop, and roll" in school fire drills, surely they can remember this!) Let me give you a more in depth description of the formula.

Stop

Whether your son is four years or fourteen, it's hard for him to stop and consider an action and the possible consequences related to the action. Some boys are by nature more impulsive than others and the exercise of stopping to consider an action will prove to be difficult for them. In fact, a recent study that examined risk-taking behaviors in boys and men ranging in age from nine to thirty-five found that teenagers took the most risks compared with the other groups. The most risky behavior was seen in fourteen year olds. The lead author of the study went on to say that the study is a first step in determining why teenagers engage in extremely risky behaviors such as drug use and unsafe sex.[1]

This shouldn't come as a surprise as the study reveals what auto insurance companies have known for some time: Boys don't always stop to think things through and, therefore, are at higher risk than others—thus, the higher insurance premiums on teenage male drivers! Just because they are naturally more impulsive at this age doesn't mean we sit back and excuse it. It's up to us to help them make wise choices by giving them the tools to build their self-control muscles. The first step is to help them learn simply to "stop," pause, or take a breath before jumping into something that can produce a whirlwind of devastating consequences.

The first step is to help them learn simply to "stop," pause, or take a breath.

If our sons are to exercise their self-control muscles, they must learn to stop and regroup by bringing the scenario before God. This is a first step to training our sons to self-monitor by cultivating the daily discipline of laying their hearts bare before God. In Psalm 139:23–24 David set the example:

> Search me, O God, and know my heart;
> Test me and know my anxious thoughts.
> Point out anything in me that offends you,
> And lead me along the path of everlasting life.

David knew firsthand the pain that can result from making impulsive decisions. If only he had asked God to "point out anything in me that offends you" in the moments that followed his witnessing Bathsheba bathing on a rooftop outside his window! Whether our boys are faced with the temptation to rudely rush to the front of the line at the church potluck, play a video game for four straight hours, succumb to peer pressure at a party and play a game of beer pong, view porn on the computer, or have sex with their girlfriend, we need to help them learn to stop and bring the temptation before God. They won't always do this (nor will we), but the key is to build the self-control muscles by moving toward the goal of cultivating a habit of exercising self-control. Every time we exercise self-control, we prove to ourselves that we can. Most important, as we look to God for guidance in making decisions, we are one step farther along the "path of everlasting life." Self-control produces freedom by teaching true mastery over temptations that come. We need to help them understand that without self-control they will be prime candidates to becoming a slave to temptations that cross their path. Learning to stop before reacting is key to developing self-control.

> Self-control produces freedom by teaching true mastery over temptations that come.

Think

The boy brain and the girl brain have distinct differences. Dr. Francine Benes, who heads up a brain-tissue bank at Boston's McLean Hospital, notes, "The male brain is not at its full size until approximately age thirty." The female brain attains optimal size during the teenage period."[2] Steve Gerali, author of *Teenage Guys* notes, "The prefrontal cortex of a guy's brain first begins to develop during puberty. This part is responsible for discernment and judgment, something teenage guys often lack. The immaturity of his brain development may interfere with a guy's ability to accurately judge safety and the long-term effects, consequences, and implications of the risks he takes."[3]

This certainly explains the blank stares we often receive when we ask our sons, "What were you thinking?" or "Did it ever cross your mind . . . ?" Bottom line: they *weren't* thinking; and no, it likely *didn't* cross their minds. However, the delayed cognitive development in the male brain doesn't mean our sons are incapable of connecting possible consequences to certain actions. It just won't come naturally for them. Our role is to help them develop the habit. It doesn't come naturally for them to want to brush their teeth either, but for the sake of teaching them proper dental hygiene, we persevere when it comes to training them to incorporate teeth brushing into their daily routine. And for those of us who don't, we often have a hefty price to pay on down the road. The same is true with self-discipline. Even though it doesn't come naturally for our sons to stop, pause, and think things through, we persevere in the task, knowing that a lack of self-control can likewise leave them (and us) with a hefty price to pay on down the road.

The male brain is not at its full size until approximately age thirty.

Learning to stop and think are essential tools when it comes to making wise choices, but there is also a spiritual component at play. Our boys need to learn the value of leaning on God for strength. They need to develop the habit of prayer.

Pray

From an early age our sons should be taught Matthew 26:41: "Keep alert and pray. Otherwise temptation will overpower you. For though the spirit is willing enough, the body is weak!" Self-control is one of the most difficult disciplines we will learn. And I dare say, many of us (myself included) are still working on it. Our nature (or our "flesh") naturally gravitates toward instant gratification and pleasure. Our sons need to know that their desire for instant gratification is normal. However, we must give them the tools for exercising self-control less they grow up to became impulsive, foolish adults who live from one temporary pleasure to another. Momentary, temporary pleasures do not produce an abundant and fulfilling life. They may appear to some to do so; but take a closer look behind the veil, and I can guarantee you, you will find misery. Enslavement to ungodly temptations always produces misery. True mastery over our flesh (sinful desires) is only possible with the help of Christ. Our sons must be taught to lean on Christ for guidance, wisdom, and strength when facing temptations.

> *O*ur sons must be taught to lean on Christ for guidance, wisdom, and strength when facing temptations.

Depending on your son's age, the temptation of the day may be resisting a can of sugary soda in the fridge that you said is off limits or reining in the urge to trip his sister when she walks past him in the family room. If he's older, the temptation of the day could be saying no to a weekend party invitation where alcohol will be available. Or clicking on a link to a porn Web site one of his buddies told him about. Our sons need to be taught that fighting temptations in their own power will often prove futile. They need a supernatural strength that can only be found in Christ. Crying out to God in prayer and asking for Him to help them will be essential in fighting temptations that cross their paths on a daily basis.

In 2 Peter 1:6 Paul sums up the formula for self-control: "Knowing God leads to self-control. Self-control leads to patient endurance, and patient endurance leads to godliness." Self-control is a by-product of "knowing God" and, as I mentioned earlier, a fruit of the Spirit (Gal. 5:22–23). If we want to raise sons who are self-controlled, we must first introduce them to God and the beauty of the gospel. This doesn't mean we drop them off at church each Sunday and trust that by default of being there they will develop a thriving relationship with Christ. Regular church attendance is only part of the equation. God has appointed us to be the primary disciplers of our sons and more will be caught than taught during the years our sons spend with us.

Our priority should not be simply to teach our sons self-control but first and foremost reveal to them the grace of God. In other words, we are to live out the beauty of the gospel in front of our children. Titus 2:11–14 sums it up well:

> For the grace of God that brings salvation has appeared
> to all men. It teaches us to say "No" to ungodliness and
> worldly passions, and to live self-controlled, upright
> and godly lives in this present age, while we wait for the
> blessed hope—the glorious appearing of our great God and
> Savior, Jesus Christ, who gave himself for us to redeem us
> from all wickedness and to purify for himself a people that
> are his very own, eager to do what is good. (Titus 2:11–14)

To attempt to teach our sons self-control apart from the power of Christ is futile. In fact, it's not only futile but dangerous. Jesus' harshest criticism was directed at the Pharisees and their focus on "behavior modification" rather than "heart inhabitation." We all have a gluttonous, self-seeking desire to hop from one pleasure to another. Yet chasing after these desires will leave us empty in the end. When we help our sons understand this paradox, it creates a beautiful opportunity to introduce the gospel of Christ and show them their obvious need for a Savior.

Our priority should not be simply to teach our sons self-control but first and foremost reveal to them the grace of God.

CHAPTER 7

Porn: A Virtual Reality

onths before I committed to write this book, a friend contacted me to share a heartbreaking story that had recently devastated her community. A group of third grade boys who attend a local private Christian school had been passing around an iTouch during the lunch hour during the first couple weeks of school. The school likely had rules in place regarding the use of phones and other wireless devices, but as you can imagine, it's nearly impossible for teachers and faculty to keep tabs on each and every student throughout the day to ensure they follow the rules. By the time a teacher finally noticed the boys passing around the device and took it up, the damage had been done. To the teacher's horror, the boys had been viewing a porn site. Like many of the newer model MP3 devices, an iTouch comes loaded with a wireless Internet browser, which makes Web-surfing possible in locations with Internet access.

Unfortunately the porn site the boys were viewing was not your average run-of-the-mill porn site. It was one of the largest online portals for homemade porn clips. Likely one of the boys had heard about the site from an older brother or neighbor kid. I doubt many of the parents had even had the birds-and-bees talk with their boys, given they were only eight or nine years old. They were children, far too young to even begin to process God's divine design for sex, much less the images that are now forever etched in their minds. Mind you, this could be anyone's son. Mine or yours. The sobering reality even for those of us who faithfully set up parental controls on our sons' wireless devices, it only takes one boy in your son's peer group armed with any device that can access the Web, a little free time, and an invitation to your son to "take a look."

Mary Anne Layden, codirector of the Sexual Trauma and Psychopathology Program at the University of Pennsylvania's Center for Cognitive Therapy, called porn the "most concerning thing to psychological health that I know of existing today." She further notes, "The internet is a perfect drug delivery system because you are anonymous, aroused and have role models for these behaviors," Layden said. "To have drugs pumped into your house 24/7, free, and children know how to use it better than grown-ups know how to use it—it's a perfect delivery system if we want to have a whole generation of young addicts who will never have the drug out of their mind. . . . Pornography addicts have a more difficult time recovering from their addiction than cocaine addicts since coke users can get the drug out of their system, but pornographic images stay in the brain forever."[1]

It's Not a Matter of *If* but *When*

Before we prepare to tackle the problem of porn and talk solutions, it is first necessary to understand how widespread the problem is. By some estimations the production and sale of explicit pornography now represents the seventh-largest industry in America.[2] According to one study, researchers at the University of New Hampshire found that about 90 percent of children between the ages of eight and sixteen have looked at porn. In fact, the largest group of Internet pornography consumers are between the ages of twelve and seventeen. The study also found that most kids who watch porn on the computer weren't searching for it the first time they found it.[3]

Consider that in 1985, 92 percent of adult males had a *Playboy* magazine by age fifteen as compared to today where the average age of a boy's first exposure to pornography is eleven.[4] Nearly half of boys between the third and the eighth grade have visited Internet sites with adult content.[5] Other studies have revealed that 75 percent of eighteen- to twenty-four-year-olds (late adolescent guys) visit online porn sites monthly, representing one-fourth of the visitors to all Internet porn sites. The next largest users of porn are men in their twenties and early thirties, 66 percent of whom report being regular users of porn.[6]

> *The largest group of Internet pornography consumers are between the ages of twelve and seventeen.*

While porn has always been around in some form or fashion, it used to be harder for boys to get their hands on it in days past. In my generation boys were usually exposed to porn with a sneak peek at a neighbor kid's stashed copy of Dad's back issue of *Playboy* magazine. Or if they were really desperate, the bra and panties section of the JCPenney's catalog. Today porn is accessible on the Internet, portable gaming devices, cell phones, and just about any gadget with wireless capabilities. A boy doesn't need to go looking for it; at some point it will find him. And what's out there today can make *Playboy* magazine seem boring and innocuous. Just like the third grade boys who were simply passing around another boy's iTouch at lunchtime, it can happen with little or no warning.

Take, for example, Susan, whose son was exposed to pornography while working on a school laptop in high school. She contacted me several months ago to share about the painful journey they had experienced. Here is what she had to say:

> *My son kept his secret for eighteen months. Although we knew something was terribly wrong, we never imagined that this was the problem. It has been a long, difficult road. We have invested much time and patience in his spiritual development to give him tools to overcome this serious addiction. I was very concerned when he went away to college this fall, but he has been faithful and by the hand of God was matched with a mentor who had struggled with the same issue and has walked a road of healing. I never expected to deal with this kind of addiction, nor did I have any idea of the long-term problems this would bring.*

Another mom, Julie, also contacted me to share her account of how her son's porn habit mastered his life for several years:

> *I have three sons and a daughter. My eldest son is sixteen, and he started struggling with porn around age thirteen. He told us he learned about a Web site from friends one day while sitting in the school cafeteria. He visited that Web site*

(which was very hardcore, by the way), and it produced a
secret intrigue to see more and more. My husband discovered
his viewing history about four weeks after he first visited the
site. For the most part we have dealt with it, and our son feels
convicted about his actions, but there have been some slipups
here and there. The scariest thing I've heard him say was,
"I knew it was wrong, I told myself it was wrong, but I
couldn't help it, I just had to look." I thank God that our
son has come to us for support, to confess, to pray with us,
etc. (and yes, we have filters on our computers). But now he
faces a new challenge: He doesn't know how to be out in the
world without facing the possibility of stumbling. He doesn't
do church youth-group activities involving sleepovers because
he says guys talk about things that make him want to visit
the sites again. I catch him averting his eyes at billboards,
artwork in restaurants, etc. My husband says this may be a
struggle for him the rest of his life. I want him to be confident
that through Christ's strength he can "be in the world, but not
of the world," but it has really opened my eyes to the amount
of pornographic or suggestive images that are really out there to
be seen. He's just a couple years from college, and I want him
to be ready to stand firm in his convictions.

I realize many of you may be feeling overwhelmed after reading
the accounts above and coming to terms with the gravity of the
situation. It's easy to feel like the situation is hopeless. While porn
is a sad reality of our times, it doesn't diminish the power of God.
As mothers we will simply need to step up our game and come
up with a new and improved battle plan. Our battle plan must go
beyond activating parental controls and telling our sons not to look
when they see it. We need to take it a step further and teach our

sons to monitor their hearts. Proverbs 4:23 says, "Above all else, guard your heart, for it is the wellspring of life." Our sons are not likely to embrace the importance of monitoring and guarding their hearts in the moment until they make the connection between viewing porn and a diminished quality of life.

The remainder of this chapter will outline the battle plan my husband and I have used with our own boys when it comes to discussing some practical dangers of porn that go beyond the moral/biblical perspective that this assumes you've also shared. They need to see the complexity to the dangers of that which is so enticing and convenient. If you feel uneasy about discussing this topic with your son, hand the book over to your husband and let him cover the information in this chapter. What's most important is that someone cover the information with him and keep the conversation going through the years. I've highlighted three dangers that should be discussed over and over again until the highlighted dangers are etched into their minds. That way, when they are faced with the temptation, they are fully informed about the trade-off involved.

While porn is a sad reality of our times, it doesn't diminish the power of God.

1. Viewing porn affects the wiring of your brain. William M. Struthers, author of the book *Wired for Intimacy*, has written extensively on the physical dynamic that occurs in the brain when porn is viewed. "Repeated exposure to pornography creates a one-way neurological superhighway where a man's mental life is over-sexualized and narrowed."[7] He adds, "As men fall deeper into the mental habit of fixating on these images, the exposure to them creates neural pathways and a path is created in the woods with each successive hiker, so do the neural paths set the course for the next time an erotic image is viewed."[8] Struthers notes that experiences with pornography and pleasure hormones create new patterns in the brain's wiring and repeated experiences formalize the rewiring.[9] It certainly brings a whole new meaning to the phrase "one-track mind."

Our boys need to know that porn is much more than a simple assault to their eyes. It affects the wiring of their brain. Each viewing session brings about a dose of dopamine to the brain (also known as the "feel good" or "reward" hormone), which leaves the viewer, much like an addict, craving more. "An elevated level of dopamine in the brain creates a high that the addict keeps chasing," said David Greenfield, the director of the Center for Internet Behavior and author of *Virtual Addiction*.[10] Greenfield further warns, "Sex is the most primitive, powerful, physiological force on the planet—it's wired into our DNA. We all have the potential to become addicted to it."[11]

As one viewing leads to another and yet another, a habit is developed (to get the repeated buzz or "reward"). As a habit is cultivated, neural pathways begin to develop that signal the brain to move down the same pathway over and over again. But the damage doesn't end there. Once this one-way neurological superhighway is created, it also becomes the pathway by which interaction with women is routed. "All women become potential porn stars in the minds of these men. They unknowingly have created a neurological circuit that imprisons their ability to see women rightly—as being created in God's image."[12]

Our sons are growing up in a culture that views porn as harmless fun. Porn is anything but harmless. It takes more than one victim by affecting the core of men's thinking and their view of women. It is not enough simply to teach our sons not to look. We need to disclose fully to them what is at stake when they make the choice to view porn. We need to help them understand that every time they practice self-control by not looking in a tempting situation, they are reinforcing a new and better neural pathway in their brain. As this pathway is developed and traveled over and over again (each time self-control is practiced), it will help create a one-way neurological superhighway that will lead them to a much better place.

I have shared these facts with my boys openly and emphatically emphasized, "Son, you just don't want to mess with the wiring of your brain." William Struthers offers this hope: "Because the human brain, the source of our mental life, is such a remarkable organ, it is important to have a good understanding of how it operates. When we understand how the brain is flexible and plastic, as well as how it is unyielding and rigid, we can see not only how pornography can lead a person to a place of mental depravity, but also how hope for redemption and sanctification can be achieved."[13] In other words, even if a habit has already been developed and neural pathways established, the brain can be retrained. It won't be easy to shut down the old superhighway and establish a new one, but it is possible.

It is not enough simply to teach our sons not to look.

Of course, it's ideal if the construction on the superhighway leading to depravity never begins in the first place, but the truth is, many boys have already begun the building process. That is why it's important to acknowledge that it's never too late to reverse the damage. I recently shared with my younger son, "If by chance, you feel a pathway has already been established, please share that with me or your dad, so we can help you begin the deconstruction process." Let's not be naïve about this problem. Too much is at stake to live with an attitude of "ignorance is bliss."

2. Viewing porn can affect your future sex life and marriage. Our boys may not care much at this point about a warning that porn can damage a marriage relationship, but I can guarantee you their ears will perk up if you tell them viewing porn can ruin their sex life. What guy doesn't want to have amazingly good sex someday? Consider this information from author Leonard Sax, M.D., Ph.D., in his book *Boys Adrift*:

> In the general population, the best estimates are that roughly 70 percent of college-age men now use pornography regularly. Among those men, use of pornography can readily escalate from an occasional diversion to a daily pastime and finally, to becoming the preferred sexual outlet. In one Harvard study, 69 percent of men who sought help for sexual problems were experiencing "compulsive masturbation"—meaning that they were masturbating more than they thought they should be, and/or they were sometimes masturbating in inappropriate places or at inappropriate times. Fifty percent of the men in the same study were described as being "pornography-dependent," meaning that they could not achieve an erection without pornography. More and more boys are discovering that they prefer a sexy image on a computer screen to a real live woman with expectations, a woman who has her own agenda, a woman who may say things that the boy doesn't want to hear."[14]

I can't help but think the above information wouldn't scare a boy half out of his wits when he hears phrases like: "compulsive masturbation," "masturbating in inappropriate places." "pornography-dependent," and "could not achieve an erection without pornography." Ouch. If our sons want to have amazingly good sex lives (in the confines of marriage with their future wives), they would be wise to resist the temptation to view porn. Of course, not every boy who views porn will become pornography dependent, but how do our sons know if they are among those who will? There is absolutely no way to tell. Therefore, are they willing to take a gamble?

Porn diminishes sexual fulfillment in men, the kind of sexual fulfillment God intended. In *That's My Son*, author Rick Johnson notes: "Porn users need bigger prizes—more degrading, more graphic, more explicit images . . . by viewing this material, a male is not exercising self-restraint or control. If he can't use self-control in one area of his life, he'll lack it in other areas as well. Boys who learn to govern their sexual urges grow up to be men who are able to engage in healthy sexual relations and are able to control other areas of their lives."[15] William Struthers beautifully sums it up, "Pornography is a sin that robs God of his glory in the gift of sex and sexuality. We have long known that sin takes hostages."[16]

> *Sin takes hostages.*

3. Viewing porn can rob you of future happiness. If anyone ever doubted that viewing porn can act as a drug, consider the following withdrawal symptoms documented in an article in *Psychology Today* from actual porn users who were trying to break free from the habit.[17]

- "Shaking w/ jitters similar to how it felt when I quit smoking."
- "Intense bouts of anger leading to interpersonal difficulties, aggressive demeanor, easily stressed out, suicidal ideation."
- "Bored? Masturbation. Angry? Masturbation. Sad? Masturbation. Stressed? Masturbation. I went from being the first of my class to the very bottom until I dropped out for good. . . . I fear I'll never have sex because I've learned no social skills since diving into porn eight years ago as a teen."

And if anyone is left doubting that porn can diminish future happiness, consider the following quotes often heard from men in the survey:[18]

- "No matter how many orgasms I have, I never feel satisfied."
- "I need extreme material that I never would have viewed before."
- "I'm more anxious or depressed, and I have a strong desire to avoid other people."

John 10:10 tells us, "The thief comes only to steal and kill and destroy; I have come that they may have life, and have it to the full". Let me ask you this: Do the testimonies of the men above indicate they "have life, and have it to the full"? Or do they sound like they've fallen prey to a thief who has come to "steal and kill and destroy"? We need to help our sons understand that a truly abundant life only comes by following Christ and obeying His commands. Temporary pleasures, though tempting, can rob them of the abundant life God intends for them. Ironically, porn is often argued as an individual's right to exercise his "personal freedoms," yet ironically, the end result can leave viewers imprisoned.

Because masturbation is oftentimes a by-product of porn, I am not going to address this temptation as a separate topic. The same principles that apply in this chapter can also be applied to masturbation. Pornography acts as a stimulant to achieve a desired buzz (orgasm usually through masturbation). Once our boys understand how habits can form neural pathways that put them at risk of locking their brains into certain behaviors, they are better equipped to make fully informed choices when it comes to masturbation. Even if they omit the stimulant (porn), they are still at risk of developing neural self-pleasure pathways if they grow dependent on masturbation. The same three dangers presented above apply to boys who become masturbation dependent.

A Final Word to Moms

While researching for this chapter, I ran across a fabulous article in the online edition of the *Chicago Sun-Times*, encouraging mothers to warn their sons of the dangers of porn. The author offered some insightful words of wisdom to mothers that we'd be wise to take to heart: "Moms, they aren't us. Rather, I think our approach to them here should be put in the context of 'of course this interests you. This is exactly how you are designed. Don't be ashamed of that desire. You were made to find beautiful women sexually enticing, and the people making this base stuff know that. But, these images aren't good enough for you. That good desire you have will meet its greatest satisfaction with a real woman, when sex and relationship in marriage go together.'"[19]

Our boys aren't like us. As a result, it is hard for us to understand the allure of porn to our boys, but the last thing they need is to be shamed with an attitude that says, "Why would you even think about looking at that?" Of course, they're drawn to it. However, this doesn't give them an excuse to cave into the temptation. It's up to parents to help their sons understand why resisting the temptation is in their best interests both now and in the long-term.

If your son is between the ages of ten and twelve (or younger if he has older brothers), you need to broach this topic with him and begin to discuss the top three dangers above. Remember, these are only conversation starters. It's important to keep the conversations going throughout the years. Even if your son is rather innocent and less knowledgeable than other kids his age, I would consider introducing the topic like this:

> Hey buddy. I want to talk to you about something. As you get older and you spend more time on the computer or over at friends' houses, you will probably see some stuff that God doesn't want you to see. Like maybe pictures of girls not wearing clothes or even two people having sex.* (Insert: "Oooooh. Gross!" from son, here.) Yeah I know, but someday you may not think its so "gross." Anyway, I just want you to know that it's important not to look if you come across something on the computer or one of your friends wants to show you something that you know God wouldn't want you to look at. And please come tell me or your dad about it, if that happens. You won't be in trouble because we want you to talk to us about stuff like that. As you get older, a whole lot of your friends are going to be looking at bad stuff and may try to get you to look at bad

stuff with them. Let's think of what you might say when that happens, OK?

(*If you have not addressed the topic of what sex is and God's plan and purpose for sex, consider beginning that conversation at a basic level if you feel your son is ready. If he's twelve or older, he's ready—trust me.)

Regardless of the parental controls we set up or the boundaries we put in place to protect our sons, our measures will not be foolproof. Our sons will eventually be exposed to porn on some level. As parents we must be vigilant in addressing the topic and the long-term effects of viewing porn. Over and over and over again.

Our boys would be wise to follow in Job's footsteps by making "a covenant with their eyes not to look lustfully at a girl" (Job 31:1). A "wellspring of life" awaits those who guard their hearts (Prov. 4:23). What boy doesn't want to experience the "good life," the kind of life God intended for him?

> *R*egardless of the parental controls we set up or the boundaries we put in place to protect our sons, our measures will not be foolproof.

We must help our sons understand that decisions they make today relative to porn can impact their future happiness tomorrow. We can't be there to monitor and guard their hearts 24–7. However, we can teach them to self-monitor and examine their hearts on a regular and consistent basis. We all know someone whose marriage/life/ well-being has been destroyed by porn. You may have experienced the fallout from the evils of porn and know firsthand that it leaves many victims in its wake. Ignoring the problem will not make it go away. We must address the dangers of porn with our sons before they walk into a snare that can leave them forever entrapped. This is a battle worth fighting.

Dad:2:Dad

Go to VickiCourtney.com and click on the link to the 5 Conversations blog for my husband's list of activities and the books/training materials he has used with our sons to reinforce this conversation. While you're there, feel free to add your husband's ideas to the list!

Not everyone's doing it!
(And other naked truths about sex
you won't hear in the locker room.)

CHAPTER 8

Beyond the Birds and Bees

When my kids were young, I had a friend who was of the school of thought that private parts should always be referred to by their correct anatomical terms. I, on the other hand, could not bring myself to embrace this teaching philosophy and therefore, provided my children with nicknames for their privates. My friend would often tease me about my nickname system and tell me that my poor kids were going to be warped for life. I wondered if maybe she was right until one day when I picked up my friend's son for a play date after preschool. On the way to my house, we went over one of those big hills that can give you butterflies in your stomach. All of a sudden, her son yelled out from the backseat, "Whoa! That tickled my scrotum!" So yeah, at that point, I was sure I was on the right track, and my friend was the one warping her kids for life . . . and mine for that matter since I had to spend the next five minutes addressing my son's question that followed from the backseat.

"What's a scrotum, Mom?"

"Uh, it's a part of your body that's right by your *willy*."

Which then triggered a follow-up question from my friend's son: "What's a *willy*?"

To which I immediately replied, "Why don't you ask your mom when you get home, OK?"

My nickname system worked just fine until one day when a new family moved into our neighborhood. I had heard that they also had a six-year-old boy the same age as my older son at the time, so we stopped by one day to introduce ourselves. When the mother introduced her son to my son, Ryan, I immediately knew we had a problem. Yes, you got it—his name was *Willy*! Anyway, I shot my son a pleading look to remain silent, but by the look on his face, it was clear that we would have plenty to talk about on the way home. I'll never forget his comment as we walked away: "Mom, why would anyone name their kid Willy?" Drat. I finally had to come clean with my son. In the end the conversation was good timing because the movie *Free Willy* released a few months later. And that's certainly the last message we want to send to our sons.

Talking about sex is intimidating for many parents and even more so for mothers who attempt to broach the topic with their sons. Gone are the days when Dad worked up his nerve to have the one-time talk with his son so he could scratch it off his to-do list. Given the culture in which we live, we need all hands on deck when it comes to raising our sons to be sexually pure. We need both Mom and Dad to take advantage of teachable moments as they occur. I know this is a difficult thought for many of you, and if you are absolutely certain you cannot bring yourself to talk with your son about sex, hand the book over to your husband and give him the task. The most important thing is that *at least one parent* address the topic and continue to address it throughout the years. My husband and I view it as a partnership when it comes to discussing the topic of sex. In fact, truth be told, I have probably had more conversations with our sons than my husband because I am with them more often throughout the day when many of the teachable moments occur.

We need all hands on deck when it comes to raising our sons to be sexually pure.

Sex Is Good—Very, Very Good

When we are talking with our sons about sex, we need to approach the topic with boldness and confidence rather than skittishness and timidity. We also need to make sure we are balanced in the way we present it, always remembering that sex was created by God for His purposes (procreation) and our pleasure. In other words, we need to leave our sons with a clear understanding that sex in the right context (marriage) is good and something God wired us to desire and enjoy. In the book *Hooked*, authors Joe S. McIlhaney, M.D., and Freda McKissic Bush, M.D., say, "Sex can be considered one of the appetites with which we are born."[1] They go on to point out that the word "appetite" can be defined as "any of the instinctive desires necessary to keep up organic life" or "an inherent craving."[2] McIlhaney and Bush say, "A truth to remember is that appetites are necessary but values-neutral. They can be used appropriately or they can be misunderstood and misused. For example, without an appetite for food, we wouldn't survive. Food provides energy and fuels our bodies. Yet the misuse of this natural appetite in the forms of overeating or eating too much of the wrong things, for example, can cause problems such as cardiovascular disease, diabetes, and many others. These health problems can dramatically change the entire course of an individual's life."[3]

As mothers, we need to be careful that we don't go overboard in our "conversations" by always emphasizing the problems associated with sex outside of marriage. If we fail to acknowledge that sex is, in fact, a gift from God and something He gave us a natural appetite for, our sons may be left with the impression that sex is bad, even in marriage. This will be especially confusing for our sons when their sexual appetites kick in (and they will!). We need to make sure our sons understand that while their "appetite" for sex is normal and natural, it is also something that needs to be properly managed in order for them to experience optimum long-term spiritual, emotional, and physical health.

Sex on the Boy Brain

When it comes to sex being like an "appetite," we as mothers need to understand better how strong the male appetite for sex is. Because we are women, we will have a tendency to address the topic of sex from a female perspective and make assumptions based on our appetites for sex. That said, get ready. I'm about to dump some candid information on you that might make you squirm a bit.

Once a boy hits adolescence, his body is undergoing changes at warp speed, and his appetite for sex kicks into overdrive. Let me put it to you this way: That same preteen boy/young teen boy who mothers commonly tell their friends is "in a growth spurt and eating them out of house and home," is also hungry for sex. Moms typically see only a boy who puts in overtime standing in front of the kitchen pantry and mumbling, "I'm staaaarrrrvvvving," but the truth is, he's also staaaarrrrvvvving for sex. I know that's an uncomfortable thought and not one you can relate to, but we must face the facts if we are to understand the challenge our boys are facing. A boy's sudden appetite for sex is fueled by a deluge of testosterone during puberty that literally floods his system. The only other time a boy experiences a testosterone wash of this nature and magnitude is when he is in utero and the embryo receives a "testosterone bath" during the sixth week of gestation, compliments of the Y chromosome delivered by his father. In their book *Raising Sons and Loving It!* Gary and Carrie Oliver write, "During this testosterone wash the level of testosterone is ten to twenty times stronger in boys than girls. The prepubertal and adolescent boy will have between five to seven surges of testosterone per day—an increase marked by a tendency to masturbate frequently, be moody and aggressive, want more sleep, lose his temper more often, be negative and critical, act like his head is in the clouds, and have a significantly greater interest in sex."[4] I hesitate to include that during this testosterone bath his penis (aka: "willy") will increase as much as eight times in size. You probably could have lived without that last bit of information, but I share it to make the

> *A* boy's sudden appetite for sex is fueled by a deluge of testosterone during puberty that literally floods his system.

point that our sons can hardly escape the changes going on in their bodies or their appetite for sex that results.

In *Making Sense of the Men in Your Life*, Kevin Leman says, "Men reportedly think about sex an average of thirty-three times per day, or twice an hour. Some people say women think about sex only once a day—when men ask for it."[5] While that might garner a chuckle or two, stop and think about it for a moment. Try to imagine how difficult it must be for our sons (and husbands) to be sexually pure when they live in a world that is all too happy to take advantage of their sexual hunger pangs. Author Rick Johnson adds, "At the risk of perpetuating a stereotype about men, there's a distinct possibility that if women knew how and what men really think about, they would refuse to be in the same room with them (I use the term *men*, but it's interchangeable with *boys* from early adolescence on)." He goes on to say: "They'd think them perverted. Guys think about sex all the time. Men even think about sex in the most inappropriate places, such as in church or at funerals. The slightest and most innocent thing—a woman's laugh, the curve of a shapely leg, certain shoes, perfume, and thousands of other scents, sights, and sounds—can set men off. During adolescence, when hormones are raging, these stimulations are intensified."[6] For those of us who are married, it's sobering enough to associate the above information with our husbands, much less our little boys! Say it isn't so!

I was recently going through some old pictures of family vacations in an attempt to sort them into separate vacation piles. My hope was that I would someday have time to put them in albums (rather than in their gallon-size storage bags). Our family had the blessing of taking a Caribbean cruise (compliments of my in-laws) that just so happened to coincide with my youngest son's thirteenth birthday. There were plenty of pictures of him blowing out his candles during our all-inclusive five-course dinner. At the time I remember thinking he still looked very much like a little boy. Oh, I knew changes were coming right around the corner, having remembered the process with my older son, but for now he was still my little guy.

Two years later we were back on the same cruise ship, thanks to a pipe that burst and flooded our cabin on the first trip and cut the trip short. We received a complimentary cruise as compensation for our pain and suffering! The pictures from cruise two were mixed in the same slush pile of pictures from the previous cruise, only something was different this time. The boy who had officially become a teenager on that first cruise was gone. As in MIA. In his place was someone who slightly resembled that boy—same color hair, same dimples, same older brother and sister, same parents—yet he didn't look at all the same. In two short years he went from looking like a boy to a new version of that same boy—a mini-man, if you will.

It wasn't until I saw the two sets of pictures side by side that I realized how quickly he had developed from boy to young man. In two short years he had overtaken both his older sister and me in height. His face had thinned out significantly, and this new man-boy even had muscles! I thought I even spotted some hair under his arms in a pool picture! And the changes weren't just on the outside. The man-boy in the later pictures was far less interested in playing shuffleboard with his family by the poolside on the second cruise. Other things were competing for his attention at the pool. I even remember hearing him comment to his older brother, "Did you see the girl that just walked by?" Excuse me? It seemed like just yesterday I was slathering sunscreen on him at the neighborhood pool and distracting him on a chaise lounger with fruit roll-ups and a drink box. Now he was sitting on a chaise lounge and being "distracted" by other things.

The short time frame where boys morph into young men is a weird and awkward season for moms. Let's be honest here. It's easier to mother a *boy* than a *man*. It's hard for us to accept that our little boys do, in fact, grow up to look and behave like men. As in the kind of "man" who might be a tad distracted when a girl walks by in an itsy-bitsy-teeny-weeny bikini. The truth is, we need to step up our conversations during this hormonal surge in addition to stocking up the kitchen pantry with more food.

> The short time frame where boys morph into young men is a weird and awkward season for moms.

Sex 101

Sex education should begin earlier than the onset of adolescence. At the end of this chapter, I have included some suggested "sex facts" to cover through the years, beginning when our boys are young and begin to have a natural curiosity about their bodies and the differences between them and girls. Once we've covered basic anatomy (Vicki style: Boys have a willy, and girls have a china. And yes, I came clean on the last one long before he entered world geography), we need to give them a proper foundation for future conversations. I love the approach that sexual abstinence expert Pam Stenzel takes in her book *Sex Has a Price Tag: Discussions about Sexuality, Spirituality, and Self-Respect*. Here it is in a nutshell:

1. Humans did not create sex. God did.
2. Since God created sex, He's the one who understands it the best.

3. Since God understands sex better than anyone, a person who wants to have great sex (and why would anyone want to have rotten sex?) needs to know what God says about sex.[7]

Once your son is clear on the basics regarding the purpose of sex and God's view of sex, you're ready to incorporate into your conversations some of the information we will discuss in the following two chapters, as you feel your son is ready. Break down the information into bite-size conversations rather than dumping an entire chapter's worth of information on him at one time. Continue the conversations over the years, taking advantage of teachable moments as they occur. A good rule of thumb to remember when it comes to discussing sex is to "keep the conversation simple and keep it going."

Somewhere between the ages of ten and twelve, children should be given a basic definition of sex by their parents before they hear otherwise from undependable sources. Some parents wait for a signal from the child before they begin the conversations about sex. This is a bit risky since some kids are quieter than others and may shy away from bringing their questions about sex to their parents. You know best when your son is showing signs of readiness, but I highly recommend that you begin initiating the conversations about sex before he enters middle school or at the first signs of adolescence, whichever comes first.

This is especially true if your son is in a public school and/or has an older brother or sister and by default has been exposed to more mature topics. However, don't let that be your only barometer. One mom recently shared a story with me about her sheltered eight-year-old son (the oldest of three children) who snuck onto the family computer and googled "what is sex?" Her husband discovered it when checking the history on the computer, and they were stunned to learn that "sex" had somehow made it onto their son's radar. When they asked their son where he first heard of sex, he matter-of-factly told them "from my friends." It's a tedious balance because we want to protect our sons' innocence for as long as possible, yet at the same time we want them to hear accurate information about sex less they be misinformed from outside sources.

When I felt it was a good time to broach the topic with my sons, I said something to the effect of, "Hey buddy, I need to talk to you about something important. At some point in the next few years, you are going to hear things about sex from your friends or on TV or somewhere else. (This assumes your son has been given a basic definition of the word *sex* by this point. If not, you'll need to add that to your conversation!) Here's the deal. Some of the things you hear aren't going to be true, and I want you to know what God has to say about sex because He's the One who created it. So make me a promise. If you hear something, I want you to come and talk to me or Dad, OK? Deal?" At that point I followed by asking my son if he had heard anything about sex and made sure he knew it was a safe topic to discuss. And yes, both of my boys admitted they had already heard something about sex at that point from other sources. Thus our conversations began.

My personal philosophy is that once boys hit middle school and are exposed to countless outside influences regarding sex, *anything* is fair game to talk about. For example, when my younger son, Hayden, was in the eighth grade, we talked about lust. I knew it was time to talk about it when one afternoon I took Hayden to get an ice cream bar at a local drugstore after school. I parked out front, handed him some money, and told him I would wait in the car. About five minutes later he emerged with a candy bar in hand.

When he got in the car, I said, "Did you change your mind about getting ice cream?" He kind of smiled sheepishly and said, "Did you see that really attractive girl walk out right before I did?" I replied that I hadn't and he continued, "OK, well I was on my way to the freezer case at the back of the store when I noticed out of the corner of my eye this really hot girl on the candy aisle. So I decided to get candy instead." Clearly the boy was in the process of being blasted with a testosterone mega-super soaker.

While it may seem odd that my younger son would be so open about noticing an attractive girl and desiring to take a second look, know that my husband and I have worked hard to foster a safe environment for him to talk about some of the changes and feelings he's experiencing. His freedom to be honest provided me with the opportunity to give him some tools to keep those "curious glances" from escalating into "full-blown lust." Author Rick Johnson says, "Lust is a constant struggle, and those males who choose to live a life of sexual purity face a mighty battle. I am convinced that most women do not understand the intensity of that battle, primarily because women are not as visually stimulated as men."[8] Honestly, I cannot begin to understand the battle my sons (or husband) face when it comes to lust and their sex drive, but in becoming more aware of the challenge, I am better able to extend them grace and understanding rather than condemnation.

And when it comes to talking to our sons about sexual purity, keep in mind that your voice will be the loudest voice your son hears, even if you think he's not listening. One survey found that 88 percent of teens said it would be easier to postpone sexual activity and avoid teen pregnancy if they were able to have more open, honest conversations about sex with their parents. Interestingly, the same study found that only 32 percent of parents surveyed believe they are most influential in their teens' decisions about sex.[9] I find it sad that most parents don't realize the power they have in influencing their kids when it coming to sexual health. No doubt they will be bombarded with lies about sex on a daily basis from media and their peers. Our sons need to know the secret to having "really great sex," the kind of sex God intended. Will you tell them?

> *E*ighty-eight percent of teens said it would be easier to postpone sexual activity and avoid teen pregnancy if they were able to have more open, honest conversations about sex with their parents.

Bonus: Sex Education through the Years

I found the following tips from the Mayo Clinic that may be helpful in breaking down the conversations according to age and level of understanding.[10]

Age 18 Months–3 Years

Children begin to learn about their own bodies. Teach your child the proper names for sex organs. Otherwise, he or she might get the idea that something is wrong with these parts of the body. (*Oops, guilty as charged here!*)

Age 3–4 Years

Take advantage of everyday opportunities to discuss sex. If there's a pregnancy in the family, for example, tell your children that babies grow in a special place inside the mother. If your children want more details on how the baby got there or how the baby will be born, tell them.

Consider these examples:

- How do babies get inside a mommy's tummy? You might say: "A mom and a dad make a baby by holding each other in a special way."
- How are babies born? For some kids it might be enough to say: "Doctors and nurses help babies who are ready to be born."
- Where do babies come from? Try to give a simple and direct response such as: "Babies grow in a special place inside the mother." As your child matures, you can add more details.

Teach your child that the parts of the body covered by a bathing suit are private and that no one should be allowed to touch them without permission.

Ages 5–7 Years

Questions about sex will become more complex as your child tries to understand the connection between sexuality and making babies. He or she may turn to friends for some of these answers. Because children can pick up faulty information about sex and reproduction, it may be best to ask what your child knows about a particular topic before you start explaining it.

Ages 8–12 Years

Children between the ages of eight and twelve worry a lot about whether they are "normal." Children of the same age mature at wildly different rates. Reassure your child that he is well within the normal range of development.

Ages 13+ Years

The American Academy of Pediatrics recommends that before they reach puberty, children should have a basic understanding of the following:[11]

- The names and functions of male and female sex organs
- What happens during puberty and what the physical changes of puberty mean—movement into young womanhood or young manhood
- The nature and purpose of the menstrual cycle
- What sexual intercourse is and how females become pregnant
- How to prevent pregnancy
- Same-sex relationships
- Masturbation
- Activities that spread sexually transmitted diseases (STDs), in particular AIDS
- Your expectations and values

Below is a chart I found in Rick Johnson's book *That's My Son* that you may also find helpful:

Discussing Sex Education with Your Children:[12]

Age	Topics
Preschool	Don't punish children for touching their own genitalia. Explain what private parts are and what *privacy* means. Explain sex differences.
Grade School	Discuss issues of procreation in age-appropriate, general terms. Discuss menstruation with girls before they enter adolescence. Discuss masturbation in general terms with boys at a relatively early age.
Adolescent	Teach responsibility and self-control. Teach that sex is not just intercourse. Teach that sexual intimacy has profound consequences. Teach that it's OK to say no to sex until they're married. Teach that sex is not the most important part of a loving relationship.

CHAPTER 9

Play Now, Pay Later

everal years ago I was caught off guard when my younger son (in eighth grade at the time) climbed into my car after school one day and began venting about a frustrating conversation he had during lunch that day. "Some of the girls in my grade are so messed up," he said with an air of disgust in his voice. He explained that he had been sitting with his friends at lunch and two of the girls in the group broached the topic of sex. It's been awhile since I was in eighth grade, but I'm pretty certain sex was not on the list of acceptable lunch-table topics. It was just understood that such topics as spin the bottle or rumors of so-and-so kissing so-and-so were saved for midnight ramblings at an all-girls' sleepover. Never would we imagine discussing such matters, especially sex, in the presence of boys.

My son explained that the conversation began when one "popular girl" posed the question, "So, what grade do you think you'll be in when you have sex in high school?" And thus the debate began as girls began to ponder whether they would lose their virginity in ninth, tenth, or eleventh grade. Lovely, just lovely. Finally my son said he could stand it no longer and piped up by suggesting the novel idea of waiting until marriage. And yes, you guessed it. He was laughed at, scorned, and shamed. "Hayden, no one waits until marriage! Evvvvvreeeeeyone has sex in high school!" the girls responded.

And such is the world we live in. A world where Hollywood, hip-hop, and hibernating parents have left our kids thinking that sex is something you scratch off your to-do list by the tenth or eleventh grade with nothing more than a yawn and a shrug. I'm not sure what was more heartbreaking upon hearing my son's account of the lunchroom conversation that day—the warped attitudes among the eighth-grade girls at his lunch table or the fact that my son had been subjected to the warped attitudes among the eighth-grade girls at his lunch table. In the end I concluded that, at the very least, it helped him find his voice and stand up for his beliefs. I can only pray that he will remain strong in his convictions even when his hormones are raging out of control and casting a vote to "go for it." How is a young man supposed to survive with his virginity in tact when he's exposed to girls who are more than willing to give it out and have marked their calendars with a deadline in mind?

If I had to sum up the culture's message regarding sex, it would match a customer review on Amazon for one of my books to teen girls. Apparently my suggestion that God created sex for the confines of marriage didn't sit well with one reader who gave my book a one star review and offered the following comments: "Ninety percent of the world's population will have sex before they are married. . . . People will always want to have sex, it's human nature!"

Unfortunately she failed to include the Scripture verse where she gleaned that wisdom—oh, but wait, there's not one. While I would agree with her that it is human nature to want to have sex, I'm not sure I follow her logic when she assumes that because 90 percent of the world's population will have sex before they are married, it must therefore be OK. The majority of Americans are also in debt and overweight, so I guess that's OK too? And I wonder if 90 percent of the population jumped off a bridge, would the reader above join them? Perhaps God created us with a "human nature" to want to have sex in order that it might be enjoyed in marriage and serve as a means to procreate the world. And perhaps 90 percent of the population has failed to follow His game plan for sex, opting instead to write their own rules for the game. When it comes to sex, the rules of the world's game are simple: Sex is OK as long as it's mutual and protected. Go for it . . . just "be safe." Your son will hear that message over and over again, day in and day out.

A Sad State of Affairs

About four in ten never–married U.S. teenagers aged fifteen to nineteen have had sexual intercourse at least once in their lifetime, according to the Centers for Disease Control.[1] Beyond high school 80 percent of college students (eighteen to twenty-four years of age) have engaged in sexual intercourse.[2] According to Lawrence Finer, director of domestic research at the Guttmacher Institute, a New York City-based nonprofit organization that studies reproductive and sexual health, "The reality of the situation is that most people had premarital sex, and it's been that way for several decades."[3] The study, which used statistics from the 1982, 1988, 1995, and 2002 National Survey of Family Growth, asked about forty thousand people ages fifteen to forty-four about their sexual behavior and traced the trends in premarital sex back to the 1950s. Of those interviewed in 2002, 95 percent reported they had had premarital sex; 93 percent said they did so by age thirty.[4]

About four in ten never–married U.S. teenagers aged fifteen to nineteen have had sexual intercourse at least once in their lifetime.

No doubt we have our work cut out for us when it comes to encouraging our sons to save sex for marriage. I didn't write this chapter to depress you but rather to implore you to address the seven-ton elephant that's sitting in the middle of the living room. We must have some candid and blunt conversations with our sons to arm them in the battle they face. God knew what He was doing when He created sex for the confines of marriage. It's up to us to educate our sons to the why behind His rules.

What the Media Is NOT Telling Your Son about Sex

Your son is bombarded on a daily basis with messages regarding sex. When was the last time you saw a scene on TV or in a movie that, after highlighting sex outside of marriage, showed one of the characters dealing with news of an unwanted pregnancy? What if the TV show or movie reflected the reality that one-fourth of sexually active teens has an STD by having one-fourth of their characters contract an STD? What if the media portrayed the fallout from contracting an STD, like working up your nerve to tell your partner or, for that matter, your future partners? Or what if the media demonstrated the finding that two-thirds of all sexually experienced teens regret their decision to have sex and wish they had waited longer.[5]

So the lie continues to be peddled day in and day out, leaving our children with the impression that sex is nothing more than a recreational hobby. No consequences, no strings attached. But there *are* consequences, and there *are* strings attached. That's where we come in. We must be diligent in exposing the lies and counteracting them with God's truths.

In addition to ignoring the fallout from having sex outside of marriage, the media also fails to address the benefits of saving sex for marriage. Think about it. When was the last time you heard a media report announcing that those who abstain from sex outside of marriage have the best sex once they are married? The Family Research Council surveyed eleven hundred people about their sexual satisfaction and found 72 percent of all married "traditionalists (those who 'strongly believe out of wedlock sex is wrong') reported a higher sexual satisfaction. 'Traditionalists' scored roughly 31 percentage points higher than the level registered by unmarried 'nontraditionalists' (those who have no or only some objection to sex outside of marriage), and 13 percentage points higher than that registered by married nontraditionalists."[6]

It gets better. A study by the National Institute for Healthcare Research found that couples who don't sleep together before marriage and who are faithful during marriage are more satisfied with their current sex life (and also with their marriages) compared to those who were involved sexually before marriage.[7] I wonder how many young people might choose to abstain if they knew that their reward would be a higher likelihood of having a lasting, monogamous, sexually satisfying marriage.

Of course, you don't hear the media highlighting any of the above data. The culture will continue to tell our sons that sex is a natural, normal part of life. They will scream and fight to abolish abstinence-based sex education and continue to peddle the "safe sex" message ad nauseam. It is imperative that we as mothers pick up the slack and share with our sons the details that culture refuses to address.

Couples who don't sleep together before marriage and who are faithful during marriage are more satisfied with their current sex life.

Unless we expose the faulty thinking behind the culture's free-sex message and the fallout that has resulted from believing it, it will be impossible adequately to address the issue of sex outside of marriage with our sons. It's not enough to tell our sons to "wait because God says so." It would be nice if it were that easy. The truth is, the message that God created sex for the confines of marriage often gets drowned out by raging hormones, peer pressure, and a nonstop message coming from culture that "everyone's doing it." Our sons deserve to know all the facts before making a decision to have sex outside of marriage.

The Fallout from Not Waiting: Physical, Emotional, and Spiritual

In this chapter I will concentrate on three areas of fallout that we will need to emphasize with our sons over and over again.

Because boys today are exposed to sex at a much earlier age than in the past, I personally recommend introducing the three areas of fallout sometime between fifth and seventh grades. If your son is not exposed to older brothers or sisters, is not socially inclined, and has limited contact with TV, media devices, and the Internet, you might be able to pull off waiting until seventh and eighth grade. If your son is younger than fifth or sixth grade, that doesn't mean you can skip this chapter! The years leading up to middle school are critical years that should be used to build a basic framework centered around God's design for sex. In other words, look at it like a building project. In the early years (pre-k to kindergarten), a foundation should be poured by addressing our sons' basic questions (e.g., Why are boys and girls different? Where do babies come from?). In the grade school years, we should begin to build the framework on that foundation by offering our sons more details to questions they may have and by developing an open line of communication (as we discussed in chapter 8). By the time they hit middle school, the prep work should be completed (the foundation and framework), so the rest of the building process can be completed. In this stage nothing is off limits to talk about, and we should be ready to react to things our sons are exposed to that openly contradict God's design for sex. In addition to taking advantage of teachable moments, we will also need to initiate scheduled conversations about sex. Notice that our position needs to be proactive. We are the builder. We should not wait for our sons to come to us (most will not) and ask us to assume the role of building foreman. Nor do we hand off the role to our sons' youth ministers and assume they will take care of it. We cannot delegate the task. It is our responsibility to lay the foundation, build the framework, and finish the project, preferably by the time our sons leave the nest. While some boys may choose to tear down what we have built once they are out from under our teaching/supervision, our assignment is to diligently and faithfully guide them in God's truth regarding sex.

The information below has been tested out on my own sons, and they are so well versed in information, they could have easily written this portion of the chapter!

Physical Fallout

Approximately ten million new cases of Sexually Transmitted Diseases (STDs) occur among young people aged fifteen to twenty-four each year in the United States.[8] One out of four sexually active teen girls is diagnosed with an STD every year.[9] Among teen girls who are sexually active, approximately 40 percent have an STD.[10] Read that last sentence and ponder for a minute the impact that statistic has on our sons should they choose to "go for it." I've pointed out to my boys that one moment of weakness can lead to a lifetime of regret. Add to the equation that most girls don't even know they are infected with an STD, and we've got ourselves a real mess. While we often hear of the devastating consequences that can result from an undetected STD in girls, such as cervical cancer and infertility, guys with STDs are not without consequences. The six most common STDs in men are HIV/AIDS, gonorrhea, chlamydia, herpes simplex virus-2, HPV, and syphilis. Some are known to cause inflammation of the testicles, prostate, and urethra (chlamydia); genital warts and increased risk of cancers

> *Approximately ten million new cases of Sexually Transmitted Diseases (STDs) occur among young people aged fifteen to twenty-four each year in the United States.*

of the penis, anus, and rectum (HPV); or damage to the brain, cardiovascular system, and many organs in the body (untreated syphilis).[11]

But STDs aren't the only possible physical consequence of sex outside of marriage. Six in ten pregnancies involving teen fathers end in a birth, which is guaranteed to change the entire trajectory of a boy's life. Author Pam Stenzel, in her book *Sex Has a Price Tag*, says, "A teen father will end up paying a total of between $50,000 and $250,000 (depending on his income) over the next 18 years" to support a child.[12] She recounts the following story involving a young man she met while doing an event at a high school event:

> A few years ago, I spoke at a high school in northern Minnesota. When I was done, a popular senior guy stood up and admitted to his classmates for the first time that he was a dad. The summer before he'd had sex with a girl whose family had been vacationing in the area. They'd had sex once. Neither of them thought they'd see the other one again. They had no plans beyond having a good time one night during summer break.
>
> He worked at a Burger King in town. Money was taken out of each paycheck to help support his baby. That will continue at every job he has for the next 18 years.[13]

She ended by posing this question to the teen guys in the audience: "Guys, what will you say to the girl you want to marry someday if you've already got a child? 'By the way, honey, for the next ten years a chunk of my take-home pay will be used to provide for my first child, so we're going to have to stick to a tight budget.'"[14] Food for thought, and certainly something we need to share with our sons in an effort to help them better understand the long-term physical consequences of sex outside of marriage, even if sex occurs just one time.

Emotional Fallout

One of the most powerful incentives to save sex for marriage is the link between oxytocin and sexual activity. What is oxytocin, you may wonder? Oxytocin is a hormone that acts as a messenger hormone that is sent from a woman's brain to the uterus and breasts to induce labor, as well as let down milk after the baby is born to prepare for the process of nursing. But here's where it gets interesting. Oxytocin is also released during sexual activity.[15] Oxytocin is the "bonding hormone" that not only connects mother and child but also husband and wife. In addition to bonding, ocytocin increases trust.[16] The kind of trust that builds confidence that the person you have now "bonded" with will be there for you. Always and forever. Until death do you part.

Psychologist Jess Lair of Montana State University describes the bonding process that takes place during sexual intercourse in this way: "Sexual bonding includes powerful emotional, psychological, physical, and spiritual links that are so strong that the two people become one, at least for a moment. Sexual intercourse is an intense, though brief physical bonding that leaves indelible marks on the participants. . . . To believe one can walk away from a sexual experience untouched is dangerously naïve."[17]

In light of the information regarding oxytocin, now consider God's design for marriage when He says, "A man will leave his father and mother and be united to his wife, and they will become one flesh" (Gen. 2:24). Other references to the act of sex bonding husband and wife as "one flesh" occur in Matthew 19:5; Mark 10:8;

and Ephesians 5:31. But what if sex occurs with someone who will not become a person's spouse? Would that same act of "bonding" occur? Consider 1 Corinthians 6:16 that says, "Do you not know that he who unites himself with a prostitute is one with her in body? For it is said, 'The two will become one flesh.'" It should come as no surprise that the scientific discovery of oxytocin supports God's design for sex: It is reserved for a husband and wife in the confines of marriage. God created oxytocin as a "glue" that helps bond mother and child and husband and wife. Sex outside of marriage short-circuits God's design for sex, triggering a premature trust and bond that likely won't last. And when that bond is broken, it is sure to produce emotional fallout for all parties. Meg Meeker, pediatrician and author of *Boys Should Be Boys*, notes that boys aren't exempt from emotional fallout resulting from sex outside of marriage.

> I travel across the country speaking to groups of teenagers about sex and its medical risks. I've noticed that junior and senior boys lean forward in their seats not when I describe the dangers of sexually transmitted diseases, but when I talk about the emotional costs associated with unmarried sexual intercourse. What I've discovered is that while girls are vocal about this sense of loss, boys are not—but feel it just as deeply. But what's more, the emotional costs of sexual intercourse are something boys didn't expect. Boys feel they were never told that sex can bring emotional hurt.[18]

In *Hooked*, authors Joe McIlhaney, M.D., and Freda McKissic Bush, M.D., note that this neuro-chemical process that takes place in males during sexual intercourse "produces a partial bond with every woman they have sex with."[19] "They do not realize that this pattern of having sex with one woman and then breaking up and then having sex with another woman limits them to experience only one form of brain activity common to humans involved sexually— the dopamine rush of sex."[20] They further say, "The individual who goes from sex partner to sex partner is causing his or her brain to mold and gel so that eventually begins accepting that sexual pattern as normal. For most people this brain pattern seems to interfere with the development of the neurological circuits necessary for the long-term relationships that for most people result in stable marriages and family development."[21]

> When it comes to the emotional health of our sons, the healthiest path is to save sex for marriage.

Given the power of oxytocin and the emotional bond it creates, it shouldn't come as a surprise that a recent study of sexually active adolescents found that both boys and girls who have had sex are three times more likely to be depressed than their friends who are still virgins. The girls who became sexually active were three times more likely to have attempted suicide as their virgin friends, while the sexually active boys were fully seven times more likely to have attempted suicide.[22] I have shared with both my boys the information regarding oxytocin, and it seemed to make an impact on them. In fact, I've been known to subject some of their friends to an oxytocin tutorial from time to time. (Lucky them!) Sex outside of marriage can bring untold amounts of pain and heartache. When it comes to the emotional health of our sons, the healthiest path is to save sex for marriage.

Spiritual Fallout

In addition to possible physical and emotional consequences associated with having sex outside of marriage, many teens also experience spiritual consequences. Children who are raised in the church and taught God's divine plan for sex know in their hearts it's wrong to have sex outside of marriage. Yet many cave into the temptation and fall into a spiral of conviction and guilt. Many will vow to stop having sex in an effort to reconnect with God only to slip up and begin the cycle again. Before long the cycle of guilt begins to define the relationship with God. Prayer time is spent confessing and asking God for His forgiveness or begging Him for strength to endure the temptation. And if the slipups continue, before long a sense of defeat sets in, and it becomes more difficult to "approach the throne of grace with confidence" (Heb. 4:16). Perhaps this is why God tells us, "The body is not meant for sexual immorality, but for the Lord, and the Lord for the body" (1 Cor. 6:13).

In the next chapter we will discuss additional ways we can build on the line of defense we've discussed in this chapter and, more important, encourage our sons to monitor their hearts above all else. The more we highlight the evidence that sex outside of marriage has physical, emotional, and spiritual consequences, the more likely our sons will begin to understand the why behind God's standards regarding sex.

CHAPTER 10

Hurry Up and Wait

*L*ast year I spoke to the girls in the youth group at my local church about the challenges of saving sex for marriage. Before I spoke to the girls, I handed out an informal survey for them to fill out (anonymously) and turn back in to me for a Q&A time at the end of the event. One of the questions I asked the sixty-four girls was whether or not one or both of their parents had talked to them about sex at any point over the past several years. I explained that this question included everything from formal sit-down conversations, a weekend getaway retreat, casual conversations while in the car, or a drive-by teachable moment where Mom or Dad responded or reacted to a media message about sex. It was a multiple-choice question to gauge how many conversations Mom or Dad had initiated over the years in regard to sex. I gave them the following options as answers: none, 1–3, 4–10, 10 or more. Out of sixty-four "church girls" present, only three answered "10 or more." In fact, a whopping two-thirds of the girls answered "none" or "1–3." Mind you, these girls ranged in age from seventh grade to twelfth grade and, for the most part, had parents who were consistent church attenders and highly involved in outside church activities (thus, their faithful attendance for my Saturday morning talk). Their questions on the survey also indicated that in spite of receiving little information about sex from Mom or Dad, they had heard plenty about it from outside sources. Given that moms tend to be more communicative than dads and, for the most part, more comfortable talking to their daughters about sex, I imagine the conversations with sons are scarce to nonexistent.

That is why I commend you for picking up this book, as it indicates a desire on your part to be a hands-on, engaged parent who is interested in initiating critical conversations with your sons. I realize the sex conversation can be an awkward one to introduce, especially when it comes to our sons. Please don't remain silent on this topic. Even if you are blessed to have a husband who has assumed the lead in initiating critical conversations with your son about sex, your voice is still important and much needed. It is not enough to drop your middle- or high-schooler off at a weekend retreat at the church and lean on the youth minister to educate students about God's standards regarding sex. You and your husband are the primary disciplers of your son in any and all spiritual matters.

Study after study confirms that there is a direct link between engaged, caring parents and children making wise choices. Don't ever doubt the power you have in influencing your son when it comes to sexual purity. One study indicated that teenagers in grades eight through eleven who perceive that their mother disapproves of their engaging in sexual intercourse are more likely than their peers to delay sexual activity.[1] In addition, the National Campaign to Prevent Teen Pregnancy conducted a survey that questioned a thousand young people ages twelve to nineteen and 1,008 adults age twenty and older and found that 45 percent of teens said their parents most influence their decisions about sex compared to 31 percent who said their friends are most influential. Religious leaders were only the most influential among 7 percent, while teachers and sex educators stood at 6 percent and the media at 4 percent.[2]

Don't ever doubt the power you have in influencing your son when it comes to sexual purity.

One study found that teenagers who "feel highly connected to their parents and report that their parents are warm, caring and supportive—are far more likely to delay sexual activity than their peers."[3] Another unrelated study found that close relationships with mothers seemed to discourage youngsters from sexual activity.[4] When talking to our sons about sex, Sarah Brown, director of the National Campaign to Prevent Teen Pregnancy, said that talk alone is insufficient. She further stated that what matters even more, especially among younger teenagers, is a relationship in which parents keep close tabs on them, knowing who their friends are and what they do together.[5] Amazing. Imagine that—deep down inside our sons feel more loved and cared for when they have boundaries and supervision.

Valerie F. Reyna, professor of human development and psychology at the New York State College of Human Ecology at Cornell and an author of the study also cautions:

Younger adolescents don't learn from consequences as well as older adolescents do. So rather than relying on them to make reasoned choices or to learn from the school of hard knocks, a better approach is to supervise them. . . . A young teenage girl should not be left alone in the house with her boyfriend, and responsible adults should be omnipresent and alcohol absent when teenagers have parties.[6]

One of my son's college-age friends shared candidly with me that he had ended a relationship with his Christian girlfriend of over three years in an effort to maintain sexual purity after having gone too far in the relationship. He mentioned that part of their temptation was a lack of rules or boundaries on the part of her parents when he was at her home. Mind you, these are Christian parents. He shared that even while dating in high school, it was not uncommon to be left alone in the house while her parents were gone. In other words, he was stunned and amazed that her parents trusted them as much as they did. And the lesson for us in this story? Christian kids have hormones too!

Christian kids have hormones too!

A Reality Check for Parents: Church Kids Are Having Sex, Too

Eighty percent of "evangelical" or "born again" teenagers think sex should be saved for marriage. Unfortunately there appears to be a huge disconnect when it comes to walking the talk. According to a study in *Forbidden Fruit: Sex & Religion in the Lives of American Teenagers* by Mark Regnerus, a professor of sociology at the University of Texas at Austin, evangelical teens are actually more likely to have lost their virginity than either mainline Protestants (denominations such as Episcopalian, Lutheran, etc.) or Catholics, and they lose their virginity at a slightly younger age—16.3, as compared to 16.7 for mainline Protestants and Catholics. In addition, they are much more likely to have had three or more sexual partners by age seventeen (13.7 percent of evangelicals versus 8.9 percent for mainline Protestants).[7]

Equally as disturbing, evangelical teens scored low on a quiz related to pregnancy and health risks. The authors of the study speculate that parents of "evangelical teens" may be talking to their kids about sex, but the conversation is more focused on the morals rather than the mechanics. In other words, we seem to have the "Don't do it until your married" part down but stop short of giving them advice based on a hypothetical "But if you do decide to have sex . . ." The articles further states, "Evangelical teens don't accept themselves as people who will have sex until they've already had it."[8] And therein lies the problem: If they don't *expect* to have sex, they aren't *prepared* to address the temptation to have sex. And if we don't expect them to have sex, we don't help prepare them to resist the temptation to have sex. In fact, half of all mothers of sexually active teenagers mistakenly believe that their children are still virgins, according to a team of researchers at the University of Minnesota Adolescent Health Center.[9] Regnerus sums up our ignorance to the problem in his book *Forbidden Fruit*, "For evangelicals, sex is a 'symbolic boundary' marking a good Christian from a bad one, but in reality, the kids are always 'sneaking across enemy lines.'"[10] Certainly this is a humbling thought for well-meaning Christian parents, many of which can also relate to sneaking across enemy lines in their own teen years.

What about Virginity Pledges?

When it comes to virginity pledges, there is good news and bad news. Based on a study of more than twenty thousand young people who had taken virginity pledges in years prior, 88 percent admitted to have broken their pledge.[11] Obviously that is bad news, especially if you were breathing a huge sigh of relief that your son has signed a pledge. The good news is that studies show that students who sign virginity pledges tend to postpone sexual activity.[12] Now I know what some of you are thinking. *What's so good about that if they are still giving into sex outside of marriage?* I concur with that thought and feel equally frustrated, yet every month we can buy is one extra month to equip them with information to support their pledge to God to wait until marriage. In addition, a study by The Heritage Foundation has found that "teens who make pledges have better life outcomes."[13] The study further found that pledgers are less likely to become pregnant (girls who are strong pledgers are more than 50 percent less likely to have a teen pregnancy than are nonpledgers) and less likely to give birth out of wedlock. Teens who make virginity pledges will also have fewer sexual partners and are far less likely to engage in sexual activity during high school years.[14]

In the study of virginity pledgers mentioned above, one group in particular stood out when it comes to success: the 16 percent of American teens who describe religion as "extremely important" in their lives. In other words, the radical believers who aren't afraid to walk their talk and are more concerned with pleasing

God than pleasing others. The study found that when these teens make a pledge, they mean it. The study further found that the ideal conditions are a "group of pledgers who form a self-conscious minority that perceives itself as special, even embattled."[15]

Another study that examined the effectiveness of virginity pledges went a step farther and matched the virginity pledgers with those who had not made a formal pledge but shared common beliefs and values when it comes to their attitudes about sex. In conclusion the study found that it was not the pledge itself that served as an effective conduit to delaying sexual activity but rather a set of common variables that seemed to be present in both groups of conservative teens (pledging and nonpledging).[16] Even though the study found that approximately three-quarters of both pledging teens and the matched group of teens who didn't pledge had had sexual intercourse before marriage, both groups reported less premarital vaginal sex, fewer sex partners, and less risky sexual behaviors when compared with the general population of young people. In addition, they reported losing their virginity at, on average, twenty-one years of age, rather than the standard norm of age seventeen.[17] The study further notes:

> Waiting until age 21 to have sex may not be waiting until marriage, but it certainly does point to a grand public-health direction that would make teens healthier and parents happier. Although the study shows there is little value to a 15- or 16-year-old's no-sex pledge, the matched group of more sexually restrained young people had certain traits worth noting, including:
>
> 1. A greater level of religious beliefs and involvement with religious activities by both teens and their families

2. Greater participation in weekly youth groups

3. Less sexual experience by age 15

4. Old-country values, in that sexually restrained adolescents tended to be foreign born, with a high percentage of Asian births

5. Fewer friends who drank or used illegal drugs

6. More negative feelings about having sex or using birth control

7. Strong sense of guilt about having sex, with a bit of worry about upsetting mom[18]

Do you see what it lists for the final trait? Again, this is why it is important for mom to have a voice when it comes to discussing sex outside of marriage. The study suggests an important message for parents: "The focus should be on cultivating the teenager's ongoing home and social environment, rather than on eliciting a one-time, easily-forgotten promise."[19] In a nutshell, get your family to church; get your kids involved in church and weekly youth group activities (where the message will be reinforced and they will be exposed to peers with like-minded values); draw boundaries to protect them (behave like a parent!); talk to them about the fallout from sex outside of marriage; and continue the conversations over the years.

Locker Room Lies

One challenge our boys face (and mothers need to be aware of) is the attitude that "everyone's doing it" and those who aren't are actively seeking a way to shed the "virgin" label. Consider the following question a young man anonymously submitted to a secular online advice forum geared to teens and young adults: "Should I feel terrible for being a twenty-one-year-old male virgin?"

Here is a snippet from his post:

I really want to have sex with someone I love. I can't seem to get myself to have sex with a drunk girl at a party, which is how everyone my age seems to get laid. Both of my girlfriends ended up breaking my heart after a few months, shortly after I told them I was a virgin. It was like they suddenly got uncomfortable and awkward around me. . . . I have to lie to all my friends about being a virgin. The only thing I think about is girls, girls, girls and how badly I want to make someone happy in a mutual relationship. I don't view sex as an achievement that I want to brag about. I just want to do it because it's something I crave intensely, not just for the physical sensation but for the emotional connections. None of my guy friends understand that though, and all the girls I talk to have boyfriends or have absolutely no interest in me, sexually. . . . I feel so pathetic and like a complete loser, that I'll be terrible at sex. . . . Is it normal for me to still be a virgin at twenty-one?"[20]

I find it immensely sad that a twenty-one-year-old young man who has yet to have sex would see it as a curse rather than a blessing! Interestingly he presents an honest assessment of the "craving" he has to experience sex for the "emotional connection." Sadly our sons will be exposed at some level to the rampant mentality in our culture that male virginity garners suspicions rather than respect. In a recent survey of twelve hundred teen and young adult males (ages fifteen to twenty-two) conducted by *Seventeen* magazine and the National Campaign to Prevent Teen and Unplanned Pregnancy, 78 percent of those surveyed agreed there was way too much pressure from society to have sex.[21] Interestingly the survey also found that guys are not being altogether honest about their sexual experience. Among the findings:

- 60 percent said they had lied about something related to sex.
- 30 percent lied about how far they have gone.
- 24 percent lied about their number of sexual partners.
- 23 percent claimed not to be a virgin when they were.[22]

As mothers, we would be wise to inform our sons to take the locker-room banter they hear from other guys with a grain of salt. Guys who feel a need to lie in regard to their sexual experience are suffering from low self-esteem and, sadly, are trying desperately to fit in with the wrong group of guys in order to gain acceptance. Ironically, many of the guys who mock and tease other guys for being virgins aren't any more sexually experienced than the ones they're teasing! Our sons need to steer clear of guys like this and find a handful of friends who are committed to the same values and beliefs. When it comes to being teased, author Pam Stenzel shares a wonderful story in *Sex Has a Price Tag* about a college student who committed to wait to have sex until marriage. As the only guy on his football team who's still a virgin, he asked an older man what he could say to his friends when they ridiculed him or mocked his decision. The man said, "Tell them you can become just like them any time you want, but they can never again be like you. That's far more valuable than anything they've ever experienced."[23]

> *We* would be wise to inform our sons to take the locker-room banter they hear from other guys with a grain of salt.

Maintaining a Positive Outlook

I realize the truths presented in this chapter may have left you with a heavy heart. As a mother who desperately wants what's best for her son, second best is often viewed as not good enough. And let's face it, "best" in this situation is saving sex for marriage. While it is my prayer that my sons will experience God's "best" when it comes to His plan and design for sex, ultimately the decision to wait is theirs, not mine. Our sons possess a free will, and many will have to learn some truths the hard way. However, that doesn't mean they are beyond God's reach or, for that matter, His grace. While it's reasonable to have high expectations for our sons, we need to be careful that we don't send a message to our sons that anything less than perfection (saving sex for marriage, in this case) is ultimate failure. Sometimes, as believers, we get so caught up in peddling the "virgin 'til your married and nothing less" message, we lose sight of the more important issue at hand: our son's hearts. With that said, I'm certainly not suggesting we present the topic of sex from the perspective that they are most likely going to slip up. In the next chapter I will discuss what it looks like to find an appropriate balance when it comes to educating our sons about sex. No doubt we are in desperate need of a new, upgraded sex talk. A sex talk, mind you, that focuses primarily on God's "best" design for sex (waiting until marriage) while at the same time also takes into account God's grace and redemption for times when we forfeit God's best. And where there is redemption, there is always hope.

Where there is redemption, there is always hope.

CHAPTER 11

A New and Improved Sex Talk

opefully by now you are convinced of the critical importance of talking to your son about God's design for sex
and the key role you play in encouraging your son to
wait to have sex until he is married. As our sons are exposed to the
"just do it!" message by the culture that surrounds them, our job is
to inform them that not everyone is "doing it." In fact, over half of
high school students have not had sex, and among those who have,
nearly two-thirds regret it and wish they had waited.[1] If the media
is going to highlight the less than 50 percent of high school students
who've had sex and paint them as the accepted norm, why don't we
start highlighting the majority who aren't having sex and paint them
as the new norm? In other words, our voice has to be louder than

the voice of the culture. It's up to us to tell our sons the truth about sex. Not only is it God's plan to save sex for marriage, it just plain makes sense. Further, our sons need to know they are not alone in the battle to remain pure.

In an earlier chapter we discussed the delayed growth in the frontal lobe of the boy brain, which makes it difficult for our sons to connect consequences with their actions. Therefore, we shouldn't be surprised to learn that studies have found that for adolescent boys there is a lag between their bodies' capability to have sex and their minds' capacity to comprehend the negative consequences of sex.[2] Let me sum that up for you: When we tell our adolescent-aged sons, "If you have sex before you're married, you could get an STD or get a girl pregnant," their brains are not cognitively developed enough to walk down a worst-case scenario path and consider the full weight of the consequences. Their bodies are saying, "Do it," and their brains have not caught up to say, "Whoa, hold up buddy! If you do it, you might find yourself popping three pills a day for an STD or paying child support for the next eighteen years." That's where we come in. We must continue to remind our boys of the consequences that can occur from having sex outside of marriage. Or as I've told my son, "My job is to act as the frontal lobe in your brain until yours is fully developed!"

We must continue to remind our boys of the consequences that can occur from having sex outside of marriage.

Both of my boys would attest to the fact that I have more than made up for the developmental delay in their frontal lobes by continually reminding them of some of the possible consequences that can occur should they cave into the temptation to have sex.

I have taken the time with both of my sons to help draw a realistic time line of events should an unexpected pregnancy occur, and I have shared a few real-life examples of young men who had to give up college dreams to support a family. While I hope my sons' primary motivation for saving sex until marriage is rooted in a desire to please God, should they get off track spiritually, I want to make sure I have given them plenty of other reasons to save sex until they are married.

Staying One Step Ahead of the Temptation

In chapter 6 we discussed the principle of self-control and the benefit of teaching our sons from an early age to learn to stop, think, and pray (STP). When it comes to sexual temptation, if they have not learned the basics of self-control before their hormone surge kicks into high gear, the word *stop* is not likely to make their radar. The Bible tells us to flee from sexual immorality. All other sins a man commits are outside his body, but he who sins sexually sins against his own body (1 Cor. 6:18). In addition to teaching them principles of self-control, we need to help them understand that the most effective way to flee temptation is first to steer clear of tempting situations and, second, come up with an escape plan in advance for times when they are caught off guard by temptation. For example, let's say your seventeen-year-old son is in a dating relationship and his girlfriend sends him a text asking him to come over and study. She then follows with another text that says, "My parents will be gone for the next few hours." ☺ Obviously, it's much easier for your son to flee at this point (by exercising self-control and choosing not to place himself in a tempting situation) rather than head on over to his girlfriend's house and attempt to exercise self-control in the middle of a make-out session. But should the temptation come with no warning, it would be wise for our sons to think through what they might say (the escape plan) in advance. In other words, get their speech down before they're in the backseat of a car with the windows fogging up.

It's not a bad idea to help our sons think through some of these possible scenarios before they occur (since their frontal lobes may prevent them from doing so!). And while we're at it, it would be a good idea to discourage them from dating girls who would be the type to entice them to engage in make-out sessions (or more) when the house is unsupervised. Part of practicing effective self-control is learning to take the time to think in advance through possible situations that may compromise sexual purity and come up with a plan of escape. The practice of self-control begins when our sons "take captive every thought to make it obedient to Christ" (2 Cor. 10:5).

> The practice of self-control begins when our sons "take captive every thought to make it obedient to Christ." (2 Cor. 10:5)

Getting to the Heart of the Matter

I realize by now many of you may be feeling a bit overwhelmed with the challenge we face when it comes to raising our sons to be sexually pure. As mothers, we like to think there is a tried and true formula that if applied faithfully and consistently will bear out a positive end result. The truth is, we can apply a formula or effective principles, but in the end we cannot control the outcome. While formulas (such as escape plans and virginity pledges) can be somewhat effective in modifying a behavior, the heart matters most. Sexual purity is not the result of a one-time pledge but rather an ongoing submission to Christ.

Mistakes will be made because our sons, like us, are sinners. When talking to youth about temptation, I often give them the analogy of coming to a four-way stop in the road. There will be times when we know that God is saying, "Go left. Left is the good and pleasing way and will keep you on My path." However, there will be times when our sons fall into temptation because "the spirit is willing, but the body is weak" (Matt. 26:41; Mark 14:38). Like us our sons will occasionally stand at the crossroads of temptation and take a wrong turn. Once they take a wrong turn, God in His loving patience, places U-turn sign after U-turn sign along the way to encourage them to turn back.

> *M*istakes will be made because our sons, like us, are sinners.

Most believers won't be able to head down the wrong road for long without the conviction eating their lunch. A true believer knows that a road of sin ultimately leads to a dry and dusty desert even if it is paved with momentary pleasures along the way. A true believer cannot justify and continue long-term in an action that stands opposed to God's commands. A true believer, who has chosen to take a wrong turn, will at some point along the way break down and cry out to God for help in turning back. True believers will express a sincere, godly sorrow (1 Cor. 7:10) as they reflect on the power of the cross and "that while they were still sinners, Christ died for them" (Rom. 5:8). Some believers turn back at the sign of the first U-turn while others travel down the road until they land in the dry and dusty desert. The sooner they recognize their sin, repent, and turn back, the better.

More important than employing behavior modification tactics related to sexual purity is teaching our sons to be mindful of the condition of their hearts. If your son does not view sex outside of marriage as a sin and, therefore, sees no problem whatsoever in heading down a path that compromises God's will, you have a bigger worry on your hands than an unexpected pregnancy or STD. A conversation about saving sex for marriage is not nearly as important as a conversation about Christ's saving man from his sins.

> *A* conversation about saving sex for marriage is not nearly as important as a conversation about Christ's saving man from his sins.

If You Suspect Your Son Is Already Sexually Active

No doubt Christian parents are in a quandary when it comes to having "the talk." On the one hand, we want to make sure our sons are clear on the why behind God's mandate to save sex for marriage, but if we go so far as to give them information related to birth control, we fear it may convey permission to mess up (or even worse, send a message that we may condone it). The finding that abstinence pledgers are considerably less likely than nonpledgers to use birth control the first time they have sex is more than disturbing. However, this doesn't mean we join ranks with the general population and rush out to buy our sons a box of condoms "just in case."

Maybe as you are reading this, you suspect that your son has already had sex, and you're left wondering where to go from here. Do not give up that battle and declare defeat. The evidence presented reminds us that there is great benefit to committing to secondary virginity since the larger the number of sexual partners, the greater the negative influence on future marriage and happiness. It could be that your son is having sex but desires to change. Indeed, statistics show that 55 percent of teen boys regret their decision to have sex and wish they had waited.[3] In this situation I would highly recommend that you or your husband meet with your son on a weekly basis to discuss the content we have covered in conversation 3. Draw boundaries, supervise your son, and hold him accountable to the boundaries you have drawn. Be picky about who he dates (if he's allowed to date), and make a point to let him know that the lines of communication are always open and nothing is off bounds to talk about. Most important, remind him that he can be forgiven of his sin if he confesses his sin and repents (Acts 2:38; 3:19). There is no need to berate our sons about their sin and shame them; that's not how God reacts, nor should we. Romans 8:1 reminds us, "There is no condemnation for those who belong to Christ Jesus."

On the other hand, if after discussing the matter with your son, you discover that he is unrepentant, and therefore not likely to change his behavior, persevere in sharing the truths we have learned in conversation 3. Most important, commit to pray for your son, and ask God to change his heart. Prayer will be your most powerful force. You cannot sway your son's heart but God can.

When talking to him, emphasize that your motive is one of concern and love. The sobering truth is that if he wants to find a way to continue having sex with his girlfriend (or hooking up), he will find a way to do it, even while living under your roof. At this point, if you suspect that he is planning to continue in sexual sin, you are caught in a precarious position. The question then becomes, Do you or do you not engage in conversations about birth control? If I were personally facing this situation with my own son and it was clear that he was not broken over his sin and, therefore, not willing to repent, I would continue to focus on God's standard and not deviate one iota. God's Word reminds us of the standard: "Be holy, because I am holy" (1 Pet. 1:16). Parents who are discussing birth control options with their sons are in a sense saying, "Hey, God's Word says to 'be holy,' but since you insist on being 'less than holy,' might I suggest a Plan B to help you cut your losses?" I could not say or do something that in good conscience may send a contradictory message to God's standards. And the truth is, if our sons are old enough to engage in sexual activity, they are certainly old enough to track down protection.

Remembering Our Place

As we wrap up conversation 3, know that there are many viewpoints among Christians regarding the most effective way to address sexual purity. It is oftentimes a heated topic that is fueled by much passion and good intent. That said, know that I am not an authority on the topic but rather a fellow caring mother who, just like you, wants what's best for my sons—God's best. And I run the same risk that every other Christian parent does.

In the end one or both of my sons could choose to reject God's standards for sex and succumb to the temptation to have sex outside of marriage. While I hope that is not the case, I realize it is a real possibility. There are no guarantees or foolproof formulas when it comes to raising sons who pursue sexual purity, even for those of us writing the parenting books. We can take the information presented in conversation 3 and use it to build a case that supports God's design for sex, but in the end our sons will have to make their own decisions.

I can attest that after having this new and upgraded sex talk over the years with each of my sons, I can honestly say that I have fulfilled my assigned role. I have taken advantage of teachable moments when we sit at home, walk along the road, lie down, and get up (Deut. 6:7). Should they decide to forego God's best for sex in spite of my teaching and instruction, I will not shrug my shoulders and say, "Where did I go wrong?" I will rest knowing I did all I could and continue to pray that their hearts would be sensitive and ripe to God's teaching. I recently told my younger son, "It's your sex life, and ultimately you have to come to the conclusion that saving sex for marriage is in your personal best interest and promises the healthiest sex life possible—emotionally, physically, and spiritually speaking. Bottom line, you have to care more about your sex life and the pursuit of godly purity than I do."

Rather than focus on virginity as the ultimate prize, we need to raise boys who are in the habit of laying their hearts bare before God on a daily basis. They may experience some slipups along the way, but their response to those slipups matters most to God. Just ask King David. In spite of his sexual sin with Bathsheba and subsequent orchestration of the murder of her husband, God counted him as "a man after my own heart" (Acts 13:22). When we help our sons cultivate the habit of guarding and protecting their hearts (Prov. 4:23), we address sexual purity

> *They may experience some slipups along the way, but their response to those slipups matters most to God.*

at the root. Fewer than 10 percent of boys will make it to the altar with their sexual purity fully in tact. Should our sons be among the rare few who can lay claim to being a virgin on their wedding day, it will not be the direct result of any trendy formula or parenting strategy we employed along the way. It will be by the grace of God and His grace alone. Fortunately that same grace is also available to those who slip up along the way. I, for one, am living proof that God's grace covers a multitude of sins and has the power to make all things new.

Dad:2:Dad

Go to VickiCourtney.com and click on the link to the 5 Conversations blog for my husband's list of activities and the books/training materials he has used with our sons to reinforce this conversation. While you're there, feel free to add your husband's ideas to the list!

Boyhood is only for a season. P.S. It's time to grow up!

CHAPTER 12

Failure to Launch:
Real Man or Peter Pan?

$\mathcal{I}$n 2006 Paramount Pictures released the movie *Failure to Launch* starring Matthew McConaughey. McConaughey played the part of a winsome, good-looking thirty-five-year-old bachelor who lived at home with his parents and was in no hurry to check out of Hotel Mama's Boy. And why would he? His mother cooked his meals, cleaned his room and did his laundry—a sweet deal for any thirty-five-year-old who wasn't quite ready to be a grown up in the big, scary world. The movie was the number one movie in the U.S. for the first three weeks after its release, grossing more than ninety million dollars.[1] Though the movie was intended as a comedy, it seemed to touch a raw nerve among many viewers and call attention to the very real problem of a failure to launch among young men in our culture today. In the aftermath of the movie, news outlets began to air real-life accounts of grown-up Peter Pans who seemed more concerned with moving up to the next level of their favorite video game than moving up in life. Whether Neverland was Mom and Dad's basement or an apartment shared with other like-minded man-boys, these Peter Pans shared one thing in common: They had zero ambition. None. Nada.

Take for example, Johnny Lechner, whose Neverland of choice is at the University of Wisconsin/Whitewater. While college might seem at first glance to be a bit more ambitious than Mom and Dad's basement, you need to know the rest of the story. Johnny-boy ("Mr. Lechner" would not be appropriate for this lad) is a perpetual college student. He graduated high school in 1994 and has been attending college ever since. On his Web site bio he brags, "I never let my schooling interfere with my education as I enjoyed over a dozen spring breaks and making numerous appearances on television shows such as *David Letterman, 20/20,* and *Good Morning America.*" He goes on to brag, "I also recently finished recording my fifth music CD, invented my fiftieth drinking game, and began writing my first of many books." Oh, and just in case you're interested, he even includes a donation page on his site should you wish to stop by and fund his never-ending college career.[2] Wow, I'm sure his parents must be proud of their thirty-five-year-old little boy!

"Youth" Redefined

While the example of Johnny-boy is an extreme example when it comes to the failure-to-launch syndrome, we all probably know young men who refuse to grow up and behave like adults.

Corporations and marketers are cashing in on the failure-to-launch syndrome, having discovered that along the road of self-discovery, these young men buy a lot of toys to pass the time. In fact, according to a study by a marketing demographic research firm, the traditional definition of the "youth" demographic is no longer defined by chronological age when it comes to purchasing patterns. "Contemporary youth should now be defined as 'the absence of functional and/or emotional maturity,' reflecting the fact that accepting traditional responsibilities such as mortgages, children, and developing a strong sense of self-identity/perspective is occurring later and later in life," the study concludes.[3]

The article recommends this disturbing bit of advice to corporations and marketers wishing to make a dime on this demographic shift: "As people worldwide delay the onset of adult responsibilities and stay emotionally and physically younger for longer, it is becoming more acceptable for older people to participate in youthful pursuits. To support this trend, marketers should routinely consider the often-overlooked 25–34 age group a part of the youth market."[4] David Morrison, president of Twentysomething Inc., a marketing consultancy based in Philadelphia, adds, "Most of their needs are taken care of by Mom and Dad, so their income is largely discretionary. [Many twentysomethings] are living at home, but if you look, you'll see flat-screen TVs in their bedrooms and brand-new cars in the driveway."[5] In a *Time* magazine article entitled "Grow Up? Not So Fast," author Lev Grossman says, "Some twixters may want to grow up, but corporations and advertisers have a real stake in keeping them in a tractable, exploitable, pre-adult state—living at home, spending their money on toys."[6]

To put the problem into perspective, imagine the outrage if churches followed suit and redefined *youth* as "the absence of functional and/or emotional maturity," rather than by chronological age. Should we take the single young men aged twenty to thirty-four who are living at home with mom and dad and incorporate them back into the church youth group? I'm sure many of these Peter Pans would love nothing more than to play Ping-Pong and engage in a few icebreaker games before the Bible study lesson begins on Sunday mornings. And with so few responsibilities I'm betting they're free to pile into the fifteen passenger youth van over the weekend for the upcoming photo scavenger hunt. They certainly ought to have the game down by age thirty-four. No wonder young adults (ages eighteen to twenty-four) are leaving the church in droves. We are no longer catering to *their needs!* What Peter Pan wants to get serious about serving Christ when his primary objective is to serve himself? Or for that matter, what Peter Pan wants to grow up, get married, and serve a wife when he can remain in the perpetual state of boyhood well into his thirties with little cultural resistance?

What's particularly confusing about this cultural shift in delayed adulthood is that national surveys reveal that an overwhelming majority of Americans, including younger adults, agree that between twenty and twenty-two, people should be finished with school, working and living on their own.[7] Yet in reality many fail to live up to their own expectations for adulthood. Which begs the question: What constitutes an official "adult"? While financial independence (no supplementary income/housing from parents) is an obvious determinant, the pursuit of marriage and parenthood were once viewed as benchmarks for adulthood. Today marriage and parenthood hardly make the radar of this budding generation of Peter Pans. Marriage is viewed as something you might start thinking seriously about after you grow weary of the single, bar-hopping, video-game-playing way of life that has become the acceptable norm. You know, that thing you *have to do* when you hit thirty-plus and your mama starts dropping not-so-subtle reminders that it's going to be difficult to chase after the grandkids with a walker if you don't get a move on it. In chapter 14 we will talk more specifically about how parents can successfully launch their sons into adulthood, but first it's necessary to gain a better understanding of the impact delayed marriage is having not just on our sons but on our daughters as well.

*W*hat constitutes an official "adult"?

The Problem with Delayed Marriage

Most young people desire to get married. In fact a 2008 report from the University of Michigan, based on a survey of twenty-three hundred high school seniors across the U.S.A., found that 80 percent say they will marry and believe they'll stay married to the same person for life.[8] Actually this number has remained fairly constant, reflecting the marital attitudes of teens over the last several decades. When it comes to the attitudes of marriage, the most drastic shift has occurred with the average age of marriage. In 1980 the median age for a first marriage was twenty-three. Thirty years later, it is twenty-seven for men and twenty-six for women, the highest it has ever been.[9]

A report issued by the National Marriage Project of Rutgers University entitled the State of Our Unions found that "men see marriage as a final step in prolonged process of growing up." William Doherty, a professor of family social science and director of the Marriage and Family Therapy Program at the University of Minnesota, cites a cultural shift as the cause for this new attitude of delayed marriage. "We've become more individualistic, living for our own pleasure—not for duty and responsibility. People have this feeling that they owe themselves a decade to have fun before settling down."[10]

Clearly, young women appear to be the real losers when it comes to delayed marriage. As their biological clocks tick-tock away, their single male friends experience no external pressures to wed. The single males have their pick of a sea of women (both young and not so young) who are bidding for their attention. The National Marriage Project report concludes, "If this trend continues, it will not be good news for the many young women who hope to marry and bear children before they begin to face problems associated with declining fertility."[11]

Is it any wonder that the number of unmarried women between the ages of thirty and thirty-four has more than tripled during the past thirty years and that the percentage of childless women in their early forties has doubled?[12] Wendy Shalit, author of the book *Girls Gone Mild*, describes this cruel irony: "Single women approaching their late twenties become more serious about the search for a marriage partner. They've gained confidence in their capacity to 'make it on their own,' and they are ready to think about marriage. However, many say the 'men aren't there,' they're 'not on the same page,' or they're less mature."[13]

According to David Popenoe and Barbara Dafoe Whitehead, coauthors of the National Marriage Project report, "A prolonged period of single life may habituate men to the single life. . . . They have become accustomed to their own space and routines. They enjoy the freedom of not having to be responsible to anyone else."[14] Among the reasons cited above as to the hesitancy of men to commit, the coauthors determined that the single most significant factor contributing to the delay of marriage is cohabitation.

As part of the National Marriage Project report, Popenoe and Whitehead surveyed single men to shed light on the reasons behind their hesitancy to commit. Consider the following findings:

1. They can get sex without marriage more easily than in times past.
2. They can enjoy the benefits of having a wife by cohabitating rather than marrying (translation: *sex*!).
3. They want to avoid divorce and its financial risks.
4. They want to wait until they are older to have children.
5. They fear that marriage will require too many changes and compromises.
6. They are waiting for the perfect soul mate, and she hasn't yet appeared.
7. They face few social pressures to marry.
8. They are reluctant to marry a woman who already has children.
9. They want to own a house before they get a wife.
10. They want to enjoy single life as long as they can.[15]

While many Christian parents are failing to talk with their adolescent/teenage children about the importance of saving sex for marriage, even more are failing to talk about cohabitation. For many parents it doesn't even make the radar until after their children leave home and they are faced with the reality of the situation when it occurs. Like a minister's wife I know, whose virginity-pledging daughter (now in grad school) recently dropped the bomb that she would be moving in with her boyfriend because "times have changed" and "everyone does that now."

For this reason we must be devoted to discussing the impact of cohabitation with our children before they leave the nest. I will be discussing the topic of cohabitation more in depth in the next chapter and include an overview of critical information we must pass down to our sons before they subscribe to the lie.

"There's a lot of fear percolating around marriage," says Hannah Seligson, twenty-seven, author of *A Little Bit Married*, a book about serial long-term relationships and cohabitation. "They want to get it right."[16] While I can certainly understand why young people might have fears about the possibility of experiencing a failed marriage, the real fear needs to percolate around cohabitation, delayed marriage, and other common (yet preventable) marriage busters. If they really want to "get it right," they need to take an honest look at the truth, rather than blindly conform to the times.

True Love Waits . . . until Twenty-Eight?

As Christian mothers, we often encourage our sons to remain pure while at the same time offer the added advice not to be in a hurry to settle down and marry after they leave home and/or graduate from college. "Enjoy being single—you have your whole life ahead of you!" Sound familiar? You may not personally subscribe to that philosophy, but you can rest assured your son will be exposed to it—even by those in the church. Let's take a minute to examine the wisdom of that advice. Given that most boys begin to have sexual urges in the late adolescent/early teen years and the average age of marriage for men is now twenty-seven to twenty-eight years old, is it really reasonable to expect our young men to fight off their sexual urges for about a decade and a half? (If you said yes, you might want to go back and review the information in chapter 8 about the male appetite for sex.) Of course, it's *possible* to remain pure until twenty-seven or twenty-eight (or older), but is it *likely*? Further, why would God give our boys sexual urges in their teen years and then command them to keep them under wraps for a decade and a half? Something's got to give here! Could it be that we have subscribed to the culture's mind-set regarding delayed marriage rather than God's ultimate plan for marriage?

William Doherty, director of the Marriage and Family Therapy Program at the University of Minnesota, agrees that a contradictory message is being sent to our children when we preach abstinence and, at the same time, expose them to societal pressures to delay marriage. "From a traditional moral and religious standpoint, if you want to discourage premarital sex, you really need to be encouraging earlier marriage," he advises.[17] As a disclaimer, he is not endorsing teenage marriages, noting they are risky. He makes the point that "when you get into your twenties, those teen risks go away."[18]

In a thought-provoking essay addressing the problem of stunted maturity among men, author Frederica Mathewes-Green states that "God designed our bodies to desire to mate much earlier, and through most of history cultures have accommodated that desire by enabling people to wed by their late teens or early twenties. People would postpone marriage until their late twenties only in cases of economic disaster or famine—times when people had to save up in order to marry."[19] Again, I am not a proponent of teenage marriages, but I do think we need to reexamine the benefits of marrying in the early twenties. I find it ironic that many young people delay marriage in an attempt to reduce the chance of divorce, yet in reality they actually increase their chances of experiencing a failed marriage by delaying marriage. Mathewes-Green notes that "fifty years ago, when the average bride was twenty, the divorce rate was half what it is now, because the culture encouraged and sustained marriage."[20]

Can you imagine the impact on the average age of marriage if girls refused to hook up or cohabitate and rather made clear they were saving sex for marriage? As one twenty-eight-year-old man told the author of a book on marriage: "If I had to be married to have sex, I would probably be married, as would every guy I know."[21] What an interesting bit of insight over the moral mess that has resulted from hooking up and cohabitation. So much for the sexual revolution that sought to bring women the same sexual freedoms as men, with no marital strings attached. In the end women are more beholden to men than ever as their biological clocks tick away while the men pursue free sex with no obligation to commit further. Please don't misunderstand—I am certainly not laying blame for the problems associated with delayed marriage solely on women. There is equal blame to go around. I am simply calling it to your attention in an effort to note the importance of relying on God's wisdom rather than blindly subscribing to the faulty wisdom of the world.

Delayed marriage makes it more difficult to maintain sexual purity. While it may be God's will for some to wait until their late twenties or older to marry and practice abstinence along the way, I can't imagine it was His plan for the average age of marriage to be twenty-seven to twenty-eight for men and twenty-six for women. We have an obligation to direct our sons to seek God's perfect will over public opinion. I am certainly not saying we manipulate our sons into early marriages. The goal of this chapter is to reevaluate societal opinions about marriage in an effort to help our sons see the purpose and plan for marriage through God's lens. As it stands, marriage is hardly on the radar on a young man's mind when he leaves home. And why would it be when he's been told over and over again to "enjoy being single" and "sow your wild oats"? Of course, this puts a burden of responsibility on parents' shoulders to prepare our sons in advance for the possibility of marriage in their young to mid-twenties. It is also our responsibility to raise them to "date with marriage in mind," rather than prescribe to the culture's mind-set that dating and sex are recreational hobbies. Given the times, it may sound radical. However, few would argue that the system in place is certainly not working. Part of launching our boys into adulthood is raising them to have a more biblical mind-set about marriage.

Delayed marriage makes it more difficult to maintain sexual purity.

CHAPTER 13

Not-So-Happily-Ever-After: Avoiding Common Marriage Busters

The institution of marriage is in great need of a positive PR campaign. Aside from the regular beating it takes on popular sitcoms and throughout other media outlets, many young people are beginning to buy the lies and see it as a curse rather than a blessing. Consider an article recently published in *Newsweek* entitled, "I Don't: The Case against Marriage," where authors Jessica Bennett and Jesse Ellison present one of the most vicious diatribes against marriage since Gloria Steinem made her infamous remark about marriage being designed for "a person and a half." (Never mind that Ms. Steinem eventually got married.) The authors begin their rant with the bold and dangerous declaration that "once upon a time, marriage made sense." The whole article went downhill from that statement, as they built a case to ditch marriage, one sad statistic at a time. Among their evidence that marriage is no longer relevant: "Having children out of wedlock lost its stigma a long time ago: in 2008, 41 percent of births were to unmarried mothers,"[1] and, "Getting married creates seven hours more housework for women each week."[2] Well, if that isn't proof we need to ditch the institution of marriage, I'm not sure what is. (Insert sarcastic eye roll here.)

Then there is the outright laughable quote obtained from an anthropologist who "studies the nature of love" and has concluded that "humans aren't meant to be together forever, but in short-term monogamous relationships of three or four years."[3] Never mind that in the same paragraph the authors hint at the root cause to their skepticism about marriage as being a part of the self-described "generation for whom multiple households were the norm . . . and grew up shepherded between bedrooms, minivans, and dinner tables, with stepparents, half-siblings, and highly complicated holiday schedules."[4] Did these two gals fail to think about the collateral damage to innocent children who are left in the wake of their faulty advice to shun marriage and opt instead to replace their partners every three to four years? While I agree with the authors on the point that the institution of marriage is "broken" on some levels, it seems to me it would be wiser to offer some tangible solutions that might help repair the damage rather than introduce an even more flawed system in its place. The institution of marriage has suffered some damage over the years, but nothing the Creator of marriage cannot heal. In a response to the *Newsweek* article, theologian and author R. Albert Mohler Jr. offered this reminder about marriage:

Christians see marriage, first of all, as an institution made good and holy by the Creator. Its value, for us, is not established by sociology but by Scripture. We also understand that God gave us marriage for our good, for our protection, for our sanctification, and for human flourishing. In other words, the Bible compels us to see marriage as essential to human happiness, health, and infinitely more.[5]

In order to be advocates for marriage, we must first identify the primary threats that seek to undermine God's design and purpose for marriage and threaten to rob the next generation of "human happiness, health, and infinitely more."

Premarriage Sex

In conversation 3 we discussed many of the negative consequences that can occur from sex outside of marriage, but there is also a direct impact on future marriage. Numerous studies indicate that when people have had sex before marriage, they are more likely to divorce if/when they do marry later on down the road.[6] According to the book *Hooked: Science on How Casual Sex Is Affecting Our Children*, coauthors Joe S. McIlhaney Jr., M.D., and Freda McKissic Bush, M.D., found that individuals who have had sex before marriage are less likely to experience marital happiness, more likely to have difficulty adjusting to marriage and less likely to experience happiness, satisfaction, and love.[7]

The book further notes, "An individual who is sexually involved, then breaks up and then is sexually involved again, and who repeats this cycle again and again, is in danger of negative emotional consequences. People who behave in this manner are acting against, almost fighting against, the way they are made to function. When connectedness and bonding form and then are quickly broken and replaced with another sexual relationship, it often actually causes damage to the brain's natural connection or bonding mechanism."[8]

Even more damaging than sex outside of marriage in a steady dating relationship is the trend of sex outside of marriage in the form of "hooking up." Hooking up is when a couple decides to have sex without any promise of a future relationship. It is also commonly referred to as "friends with benefits." Hooking up is portrayed as the norm in everything from pop song lyrics to popular TV shows and movies for teens. And thanks to the sexual revolution that rallied women to pursue sex as a recreational hobby, there is no shortage of girls willing to hook up with our sons. Of course, one would hope Christian boys are different, but the truth is, they're fighting the same raging hormones as the non-Christian boys. I'm not justifying it but rather calling it to your attention as a necessary talking point. It's awfully difficult to resist something that promises instant pleasure and is free for the taking. But is it really free, or does it come with a price?

According to the book *Hooked*, "Sex is the most intimate connection we can have with another person" and "requires the integration of all we are into that sexual involvement—our love, our commitment, our integrity, our bodies, our very lives—for all of our years. If sex is less than this, it is just an animal act, and in some ways we are performing like creatures because we are not practicing it as full human beings. Sex of this type can make a person 'feel' close to their

> Our sons need to know that the true long-term winners are those who protect and guard their purity.

sexual partner when truly they are not close at all. Sex devoid of relationship focuses on the physical and can actually inhibit the best kind of growth in intimacy."[9] While hooking up is often rewarded with high-fives in the locker room, our sons need to know that the true long-term winners are those who protect and guard their purity and, thus, the health and well-being of their future marriages.

Shacking Up: PreMarriage Courtship?

Since 1960 the number of unmarried couples who live together has increased more than tenfold.[10] What was considered immoral and unacceptable fifty years ago has now shifted to become somewhat of an expectation, especially among men. The study by the National Marriage Project found that most of the participants view cohabitation in a favorable light, and almost all the men agreed with the view that a man should not marry a woman until he has lived with her first.[11] Nearly 70 percent of those who get married lived together first.[12]

So, what is the appeal or the reasoning behind the decision to shack up? The study above sheds light on the three most common reasons cited by unmarried singles in the study above:[13]

- They hope to find out more about the habits, character, and fidelity of a partner.
- They want to test compatibility, possibly for future marriage.
- They want to live together as a way of avoiding the risks of divorce or being "trapped in an unhappy marriage."

There seems to be much confusion and miscommunication regarding any "perceived" benefits of cohabitation. Ironically cohabitation actually increases the risk that the relationship will break up before marriage. A National Marriage Project report states that "many studies have found that *those who live together before marriage have less satisfying marriages* and a considerably higher chance of eventually breaking up." One reason is that people who cohabit may be more skittish of commitment and more likely to call it quits when problems arise. Additionally the act of living together may lead to attitudes that make happy marriages more difficult. The findings of one recent study, for example, suggest, "There may be less motivation for cohabitating partners to develop their conflict resolution and support skills."[14] Those who do go on to marry have higher separation and divorce rates.[15] And whether they go on to marry their cohabitation partner or someone else, they are more likely to have extramarital affairs. When it comes to staying faithful, married partners have higher rates of loyalty every time. One study done over a five-year period, reported in *Sexual Attitudes and Lifestyles*, indicates 90 percent of married women were monogamous compared to 60 percent of cohabiting women. Statistics were even more dramatic with male faithfulness: 90 percent of married men remained true to their brides, while only 43 percent of cohabiting men stayed true to their partners.[16] Additionally those who choose cohabitation under the assumption that the sex will be better than "married" sex should take note: According to a large-scale national study, *married people have both more and better sex than do their unmarried counterparts.*

Cohabitation actually increases the risk that the relationship will break up before marriage.

Not only do they have sex more often, but they enjoy it more, both physically and emotionally.[17]

The verdict is in: Living together before marriage is damaging to a person's physical, spiritual, and emotional health and can impact the health of his future marriage whether he ends up marrying the woman he lives with or someone else. Yet young men continue to buy the culture's lies, never questioning the error of their ways and the fallout it may produce in the years to come. We have a responsibility to raise our sons to be the kind of young men who view women through the eyes of God and treat them with dignity and respect. I encounter many moms who are concerned about the aggressiveness of young women, but we need to be equally concerned about the young men (including those in the church) who are happy to play along.

Divorce: A House Divided

Nearly half of all marriages will end up in divorce. Surprisingly the divorce statistics remain about the same for Christians as they do for non-Christians. While most every parent is somewhat familiar with that statistic, few are actually talking over the consequences of divorce with their children. Of course, when you consider that nearly half of the parents are (or have been) divorced, it is understandable that broaching the topic could be awkward and uncomfortable, to say the least. However, if we truly want our sons to experience God's best in marriage, we must educate them to the damaging consequences of divorce. I think most parents would agree that divorce is far too common in our culture today, and, due to its ready availability, many couples rush into the decision. As most of us know, every marriage will experience ups and downs.

Research using a large national sample of people found that 86 percent of people who were unhappily married in the late 1980s who opted to stay in the marriage indicated when interviewed five years later that they were happier. Further, three-fifths of the formerly unhappily married couples rated their marriages as either "very happy" or "quite happy."[18] It certainly makes you wonder how many marriages could be salvaged if couples were not so quick to rush into divorce.

Far too often we hear that a couple has decided to divorce because they "are no longer in love," "are incompatible," or "have irreconcilable differences." For Christians, Scripture clearly states that the only support for divorce is in the case of infidelity or when an unbelieving partner walks away. However, in many of these cases, the marriages can still be saved with the help of counseling.

We all know of couples where one partner is willing to do whatever it takes to make the marriage work, but for whatever reasons the other partner is not. I have several friends who fall into this category, and my heart breaks for them and the pain they have experienced. They would be among the first to share that divorce produces devastating consequences for all involved. If you are reading this and have experienced divorce, I encourage you to put aside the reasons behind your own divorce and have a candid and honest discussion with your son(s) about the consequences of divorce. I doubt that any divorced mother would want her sons someday to become part of the divorce statistics. There are certain key factors that decrease the likelihood of divorce. As mothers, we owe it to our sons to make sure they are aware of the following factors.

10 Proven Factors That Will Decrease the Likelihood of Divorce

1. Save sex for marriage.
2. Have a strong foundation of Christian faith and values and marry someone with the same foundation of faith and values.
3. Do not even consider divorce as an option and refuse to make it a part of your vocabulary.
4. Get a college education.
5. Do not marry as a teen.
6. Understand that every marriage will come with difficulties. Seek to serve more than be served.
7. Understand that love is not a feeling but a commitment.
8. Do not live together prior to marriage.
9. Have children after you are married. (Note: Should pregnancy occur outside of marriage, the right thing to do is have the child. Abortion should not be an option.)
10. Refuse to settle for anyone less than God's best.

If Your Son Is from a Divorced Home

Judith Wallerstein, a well-known authority who has written on the impact of divorce on children, studied 131 people who, as children, experienced the divorce of their parents. In her landmark report, *The Unexpected Legacy of Divorce*, she says: "Divorce is a life-transforming experience. After divorce, childhood is different. Adolescence is different. Adulthood—with the decision to marry or not and have children or not—is different. Whether the final outcome is good or bad, the whole trajectory of an individual's life is profoundly altered by the divorce experience."[19] I am not sharing this information to berate divorced people. As I mentioned before, I have friends who have experienced divorce and honestly did not want it or see it coming. My heart aches for anyone who has experienced divorce. However, I feel it's necessary to address the impact divorce has on children in order to be better equipped in having the necessary conversation with our sons regarding the truth about divorce. We must do everything in our power to spare our sons from the painful consequences of divorce.

A New PR Campaign for Marriage: The Good News No One's Talking About

Most teens say they expect to marry (77 percent of boys; 84.5 percent of girls) and they further list "having a good marriage and family life" as "extremely important" (70 percent of boys; 82 percent of girls).[20] Unfortunately our young people will hear little about the benefits of marriage. When was the last time you heard the media address the overwhelming and consistent findings by such reputable sources as the *Journal of Marriage and the Family* and the *American Journal of Sociology* that "married persons, both men and women, are on average considerably better off than all categories of unmarried persons (never married, divorced, separated, and widowed) in terms of happiness, satisfaction, physical health, longevity, and most aspects of emotional health?"[21] Given that God created marriage, should it really come as a surprise that marriage is, in fact, good for us?

Mothers, it's up to us to extol the benefits of marriage to our sons as a God-ordained union that can bring much happiness and, most important, honor to Him. The National Marriage Project states that the burden of changing attitudes about marriage rests with *parents*. "Contrary to the popular notion that the media is chiefly responsible for young people's attitudes about mating and marriage, available evidence strongly suggests that young people get many of their ideas and models of marriage from parents and the parental generation."[22] That's the good news.

The bad news is that the same study also found that "many parents have had almost nothing good to say about marriage and often say nothing at all," claiming the negativism and/or silence could be due to "the parental generation's own marital problems and failures."[23]

The burden of changing attitudes about marriage rests with *parents.*

Further, when polling young people about their attitudes regarding marriage, many in the study have unfortunately grown up with unhappily married or divorced parents. They have no baseline for determining what a healthy marriage even looks like and have therefore been left with a tainted picture. Some even described a good marriage as "the opposite of my parents."[24] Ouch. Moreover, a number of participants in the study said they received "no advice" or "mainly negative advice" about marriage from their "parents and relatives."[25] Reading that last statement should cause a collective shudder among us all. How can we break the chains of this dysfunctional cycle when many are, in fact, perpetuating and encouraging it? No doubt many reading this have experienced their fair share of hurt and pain in marriage. No one ever said marriage was easy. But can we put aside any hurt and pain we may have experienced and instead focus on God's intent for marriage? In the book *Boys Should Be Boys,* author and physician Meg Meeker notes, "The most important decision a man makes in his life (aside from ultimate questions about God) isn't choosing his college, his career, or what city he's going to live in. It's choosing his mate. If a man's marriage is good, life is good. He can lose his job, a child, a home, but if he has a solid relationship with a spouse, he draws strength from it to endure the hardships. If, on the other hand, the relationship is tumultuous and painful, life feels bad. His job leaves him feeling less satisfied, his interests in hobbies wane, and he is more likely to give up hope in all other areas of his life. One of the greatest gifts we can give our boys is preparation for marriage, if marriage is going to be part of their lives."[26]

I know this is a tricky balance and will require moms who have not experienced the kind of marriage God intended to be blatantly honest with their sons and say, "You know honey, I realize that Dad and I haven't modeled (didn't model) the best marriage to you, but the truth is, God intended marriage to be a wonderful thing." It may mean putting pride aside and even pointing out others' healthy marriages that could perhaps serve as tangible examples to our sons. It might even be necessary to confess mistakes you may have made in an effort to dissuade your son from making the same mistakes. The problem is that too many with broken marriages are claiming marriage, in general, is the mistake. We must distinguish that God doesn't create mistakes, but people, in fact, make mistakes. Most failed marriages can be traced back to mistakes made by both spouses and a failure on the part of both spouses to adhere to God's standards of marriage. When these standards are not followed, marriages can suffer and sometimes even fail. If this is your case, can you accept responsibility for your mistakes and still speak highly about the institution of marriage when talking to your son(s)? Of course, if you are a Christian who is married to an unbeliever, you can point out to your son God's counsel for Christians not to be "unequally yoked" (2 Cor. 6:14). (This needs to be done in a manner that would not dishonor your husband.) God can heal any marriage, and prayer is an essential part of that process.

I realize others may be reading this who followed God's standards and, for whatever reason, your once godly husband chose to walk away or chase after a life of sin. I personally know several women who experienced this painful misfortune, and it is heartbreaking. Even though they have had a sour experience, they have not allowed the experience to sour their attitudes regarding marriage. They have worked hard to speak highly of marriage and make sure their sons are not left with a negative impression of marriage. This is an especially tricky balance when it comes to pointing out mistakes made by the other spouse; I caution you that if this is your situation, please refrain from sharing too many details or divulging information that could put a strain on the relationship your son has with his father.

We must distinguish that God doesn't create mistakes, but people, in fact, make mistakes.

For those of us who currently have healthy marriages, have we done our part in talking up marriage in the hearing of our sons? Do our sons know how much we value marriage? Do they see us exhibit affection and swap caring words? Do they witness positive examples of conflict/resolution and confession/forgiveness? Trust me, I am personally convicted by the weight of those words. I love being married. Sure, it's tough at times, and my husband and I have had our fair share of bumps along the way, but I wouldn't trade it for anything. Marriage is a gift from God. Moms, if we want to see a new PR campaign for marriage take place, it will start in our own homes . . . beginning with us.

CHAPTER 14

Boyhood to Manhood: A Successful Launch Plan

magine for a minute that your teenage son (just pretend if yours isn't there yet!) received an invitation from NASA to join the space shuttle astronauts on their next scheduled mission to outer space. Now imagine that it just so happens this mission is due to leave the following day. Would you let him go? Obviously much preparation precedes a mission, and your son would not be prepared. As crazy as it would be for your son to go on that mission, most boys are launched into the real world with little, if any, preparation and training. Do you have a formal launch plan in place to move your son out of the nest and into the real world? Or is your boy on the self-paced program—you know, the one where you toss him out at age eighteen with a wing and a prayer, hoping he doesn't show back up on your doorstep months later with a duffel bag, unable to survive in the real world.

As ridiculous as it sounds, the majority of parents have no formal launch plan in place for their sons. Meg Meeker, M.D., says, "The biggest mistake we make with adolescent boys is forgetting that they all need help moving out of adolescence. Millions of boys grow older, but few become men. No boy really wants to stay in the banal world of perpetual adolescence, but he needs someone to lead him out. His deepest longings pressure him toward manhood, and he needs to respond. He wants to respond but he simply doesn't know how. So help him. Be there to challenge him. Make him a little uncomfortable by stretching his intellect and demanding maturity."[1]

The majority of parents have no formal launch plan in place for their sons.

The truth is, our boys need help moving into manhood. Few are "growing up" and statistics support that stark reality. Consider what one modern-day single woman had to say in an article she authored for a men's magazine entitled "Babes in Boyland." The blurb reads, "Women are charging out of college, determined to take on the world—with or without a guy at their side, even when the time comes to raise a family. Are men prepared to meet the challenge?" She begins the article by reflecting on a trip to Mexico with a girlfriend. They desperately wanted their boyfriends to join them, but the author says, "They are stuck at home, short on cash—as usual. This happens a lot. Though we're hardly what you'd call fast-trackers . . . we still outearn the men we love, who are talented and smart but, let's say, motivationally challenged, career development-wise."[2] The article presents daunting statistics that reveal more women than men attend college today (fifty-six women for every forty-four men), women college graduates start working sooner than their male counterparts, and job status and security now matter more to young women than their male peers. "We're speeding along life's highway, and our men aren't even on the ramp yet . . . While you're sowing your wild oats, listening to terrible music, and letting the dishes pile up in the sink, we've begun building careers and 401(k)s. We're buying cars, applying for mortgages, and generally behaving like gown-ups."[3]

Our boys need help moving into manhood.

Another single woman shares her concern for the lack of male "grown-ups" with Dr. Leonard Sax, author of the book *Boys Adrift:*

Dear Dr. Sax,

As a 29-year-old woman, I'm smack in the middle of the "failure to launch" generation. I grew up in Northern Virginia. I went to my 10-year high school reunion last year. All of the girls I went to school with have moved out, gone to college, gotten real jobs, etc. Almost all the boys live at home, have menial jobs, and don't know what they want out of life.

I think the boys' laziness started in high school. Honestly I think at least some of the blame lies with parents. All the girls had curfews in high school. We all had to tell our parents where we were at all times. We had to keep our grades up. Not a single boy I knew had a curfew. Most were allowed to slack off in school because they had "difficulty focusing" or they were diagnosed with "sensory integration disorder." The girls had jobs at the mall. The boys got allowances from Mom and Dad. Even within the same family, there were different rules for boys and girls.

Now we've reaped what we've sown. The girls have discipline. The boys have PlayStations.[4]

Another woman, Sharon S., writes:

I'm newly divorced. I'm not sure I want to remarry. There just aren't any worthwhile men out there. My generation of men aren't looking for partners—they're looking for a new Mommy. I'd much rather be on my own than be with a man who can't stand on his own two feet.[5]

The Launchpad

In a fabulous column entitled, "What If There Are No Grown-ups?" theologian, R. Albert Mohler Jr. makes the following point:

In days gone by, children learned how to be adults by living, working, and playing at the parents' side. The onset of age twelve or thirteen meant that time was running out on childhood. Traditional ceremonies like the Jewish Bar Mitzvah announced that adulthood was dawning. This point would be clearly understood by the young boy undergoing the Bar Mitzvah. By the time his body was fully formed, he would be expected to do a full day's work. He could expect to enter the ranks of full-fledged grownups soon after and marry in his late teens. Childhood was a swift passageway to adulthood, and adulthood was a much-desired state of authority and respect.[6]

We must be purposeful in helping our sons make the transition from boyhood into manhood before they leave home. We must clearly verbalize the expectations that come with manhood, and we must show them what is involved in this rite of passage. In spite of the fact that our sons will grow up in a culture where women no longer count on them to provide, we must help our sons realize that God still does. And practically speaking, we must put our sons to work. It will do little good if action does not follow instruction.

Dr. Leonard Sax says, "The definition of adulthood is not how you spend your money, rent vs. ownership, and so forth. The definition of adulthood, I believe, is being independent of your parents. You can live in a tent in a forest and not pay any rent at all. But if your room and board are subsidized by your parents, you are still a child, no matter what your age. My concern is that we are seeing many more young men who seem to value being comfortable and well-fed over being independent and grown-up."[7]

> We must be purposeful in helping our sons make the transition from boyhood into manhood before they leave home.

As mothers, we must recognize that the most loving thing we can do for our boys is to increase their responsibilities and decrease their comforts as they get older. Boys whose mothers continue to do their laundry, cook their meals, make their haircut appointments, and manage their lives will hardly be motivated to leave the nest. What boy wants to leave the creature comforts he has grown accustomed to? Why grow up and become financially independent when you can stay up until 3:00 a.m. playing your favorite online video game and sleep 'til noon the following day, cocooned in your Spider-Man bedsheets? But the biggest argument for launching our sons into the real world is that it is *biblical*. Genesis 2:24 reminds us of the goal: "For this reason a man will leave his father and mother and be united to his wife, and they will become one flesh." The goal has always been to raise sons who leave and cleave. Not stay and play.

Times have changed. While age eighteen is no longer the accepted norm that signals adulthood, this doesn't mean we wholeheartedly embrace the culture's attitude regarding delayed adulthood. Opinions vary on when a boy should become a man as we've discussed earlier, but one thing is for certain: Preparing them to launch is a process that begins much earlier than age eighteen. The home is the launchpad, and you and your husband (if you are married) are in charge of the mission. In a nutshell, you have eighteen to twenty-two years to launch your son into the world to become a responsible, independent member of society. In other words, you have eighteen to twenty-two years to grow your boy into a real man rather than a Peter Pan. A successful launch comes in three stages: prelaunch; test launch; and final launch.

Prelaunch: The stage of a boy's life from age two to fourteen should be viewed as the prelaunch phase. During this stage critical life skills should be introduced, as well as the training required over the years to help your son master life skills. Skills such as personal responsibility for belongings, money management, goal setting, time management, and a strong work ethic can be introduced at a young age and cultivated over the years. For example, my husband did an amazing job in training our children from a young age with basic money management skills. Beginning in their preschool years, he taught them to set aside money for tithing, savings, and spending. (He followed a simple model of giving them an amount that was twice their age each month.) Each child had three plastic containers that served as their bank vault. To give them a sense of a strong work ethic, they were given chores from an early age that matched their level of ability. Some chores could earn them extra money while others were performed without pay to teach them the value of teamwork and doing their part to keep the family going.

Test Launch: The stage of a boy's life from age fourteen to eighteen should be viewed as the test launch phase. During the test launch stage, your son should be becoming more independent as he exercises the key life skills. During this stage he will have to learn some painful lessons as you begin to wean him from dependence on you and give him ownership and personal responsibility. Also during this time most moms have a tendency to come to the rescue of their sons and bail them out of consequences from their sons' sinful or poor decisions. Moms need to allow their sons to learn the higher lesson by refusing to rescue them from the consequences that may result. In the real world no one will rescue them from consequences that come as a result of laziness and irresponsibility. It's much less painful for them to learn the lesson while under your roof than years later when their actions can affect their entire family (spouse and children). For example, when each of my sons began driving at sixteen, my husband was clear on the expectations of car ownership. They were given used cars and told they would have to earn money for gas. We paid for the insurance, but we made clear that if they received a ticket or had an accident, they had to pay for the ticket, defensive driving course, and any amount required to repair the vehicle. But that's not all. We also told them they would have to pay any subsequent monthly increase in our insurance premium that resulted from their ticket/accident or lose the car.

My younger son (seventeen at the time I write this) was issued a speeding ticket just a couple of weeks ago and experienced the pain of watching over more than one hundred dollars disappear from his savings account to pay for an online defensive driving course to cover the ticket and prevent the insurance premium from increasing. He had a minor fender bender about a year ago that left his back bumper slightly dented with the paint rubbed off that he has yet to be able to afford to have it repaired. The way we look at it, the damage on our bumper is not our problem. Should he continue to have accidents and receive tickets that cause our insurance to increase, we will take the car back if he is not able to cover the costs and suggest he check out the city bus routes for transportation. We also did not nag or remind him about taking the online defensive driving course. If he didn't have the incentive to follow through, we were prepared to follow through by drawing the amount needed from his savings account to cover the ticket and subsequent increase in insurance. Several days ago he was on the computer in the next room and cried out, "Mom, this online defensive driving course is so lame!" I promptly yelled back, "Not nearly as lame as getting a second job to pay for the increased insurance premiums or losing your car!"

Final Launch: The stage of a boy's life from age eighteen to twenty-two should be viewed as the final launch phase. At some point during this stage a boy should become independent of his parents and become a responsible member of society. While some parents may hold the view that age eighteen signals true adulthood, others may feel it is a bit older, especially if college is a part of the plan. Regardless of whether you aim for eighteen or twenty-two, anything much older than twenty-two will increase the chances of a failure to launch. Dr. Leonard Sax notes:

> My own belief, based in part on my twenty years of medical practice, is that if parents continue to shelter their adult child after the age of twenty-one years, the parents may make it less likely that the adult child will ever be willing and able to meet the challenges of the real world. Of course one has to make reasonable distinctions. If your son has just graduated from college and he's 22 or 23, looking for a job, I see no harm in his living at home while he's conducting his job search—provided that you and he have discussed, openly and up front, how long this situation can last before you will expect him to find some kind of part-time job to help pay his expenses. One month? Fine. One year? Too long.[8]

Prior to the final launch, parents should help their sons project the future and weigh the possibilities, all the while making the objective clear: *You need to be independent by the age of* ___ (whatever age you determine is reasonable). Some boys are not cut out for college and would perhaps do better with vocational training. In *Boys Adrift*, Dr. Sax again notes:

> Forty years ago, even thirty years ago, there was no shame in a young man choosing a career in the trades. Beginning in the early 1980s—and particularly after publication of the *Nation at Risk* report in 1983—a consensus grew in the United States that every young person should go to college, regardless. "Vocational education" lost whatever prestige it had, and came to be viewed in some quarters very nearly

as a dumping ground for the mildly retarded. Principals and superintendents began to see classes in auto mechanics or welding as expensive diversions from the school's core mission of ensuring that every student would go on to college.[9]

However, vocational training is making a comeback as society realizes that many young people lack the funds and/or ambition to attend college. In addition, there is a demand for many specialty vocations that don't require a college degree. A *Time* magazine article entitled "Grow Up? Not So Fast," that addressed the problem of delayed adulthood among men, recently reported a surge in apprenticeship programs that give high school graduates a cheaper and more practical alternative to college.

In 1996 Jack Smith, then CEO of General Motors, started Automotive Youth Educational Systems (AYES), a program that puts high school kids in shops alongside seasoned car mechanics. More than 7,800 students have tried it, and 98% of them have ended up working at the business where they apprenticed. "I knew this was my best way to get into a dealership," says Chris Rolando, 20, an AYES graduate who works at one in Detroit. "My friends are still at pizza-place jobs and have no idea what to do for a living. I just bought my own house and have a career."[10]

If you recognize in advance that your son is not a candidate for college and would be better suited for a vocational career, it's not a bad idea to expose him to training opportunities by the age of sixteen, while he is still under your roof. One friend of mine who has three sons required her sons to learn a trained vocational skill in their late high school years in addition to their college education that followed. I thought this was a wonderful idea and wish I had thought to do this with my own boys, as a back-up plan to make them more marketable in a tough economy. As it stands, my sons have opted to attend college but not without clear expectations set forth as to what we expect as a return on our investment. In fact, my husband drew up a contract for each of our three children and required them to sign it before we would agree to send them to college. While we required our children to work in the summer months and earn money toward some college expenses, we were able to pay for the bulk of their college expenses and made clear that in doing so their college education is a privilege and not a right. In other words, should they not fulfill their end of the contract, the funding for college would cease.

In the contract my husband detailed what exactly we would cover over a four-year period. Should they not finish in a four-year period, they would need to secure a loan to pay for the remainder of their college education. My oldest son recently graduated (in four and a half years) and, as per the contract agreement, secured a loan (on his own) to pay for the last semester. He also had to cover tuition, books, and living expenses. The contract also required that each child take a minimum of fifteen hours/semester; earn a minimum GPA (determined based on each child's academic potential); remain consistently involved in a local church and Bible study while in college; and involvement in wholesome extracurricular activities, such as Christian clubs and intramural sports. Should one of our children flunk a course, the child would have to pay us back the entire amount for the course. In addition, at the end of the four-year period, a penalty fee would be required should they not meet the minimum required GPA, based on how much it fell below the preestablished goal.

I realize this may seem harsh to some reading this, but my husband and I are of the school of thought that college educations are a privilege, not a right, and college is not a season of life where young people are supposed to "sow their wild oats." While the contract did not detail a specific moral code of conduct for behavior, it was more than understood that should pictures pop up on Facebook showing our child engaged in a game of beer pong, slamming down vodka shots, or engaging in other dangerous or sinful behaviors, it's time for the child to come home. And by "come home," we mean, come home and pay for rent, get a job, with the option to enroll at the local community college (on their dime). For the amount we are paying for college, we have every right and an obligation to attach strings to the dollars we are fronting as an investment toward their future. I'm happy to say that our two older children, who are already at this stage of life, have in general made wonderful choices regarding their peer groups in college and their involvement in Christian activities and plugged into a fabulous church. The contract successfully served as a motivation to stay on the right path.

In addition to preparing our children for the final launch phase, we have also had many conversations related to the downside to delayed marriage. We have also discouraged our children from dating for recreation (the culture's model) and encouraged them instead to date with marriage in mind. (I will discuss this concept more in depth in chapter 16.)

Tough Love

Every child is different, and the system my husband and I have used with our boys may not be the best system for your son(s). The main thing is to have a launch plan for your son(s) in place and let him clearly know what your expectations are. You may have to revise and tweak it along the way, but don't give in and postpone the launch indefinitely. One friend of mine has a son who experienced a "failure to launch." He went to college upon graduating from high school and came home after one year on scholastic probation. He went back for another try and flunked out completely. Back home and living in his room, he secured a part-time job and registered for a few courses at a local community college. He stayed up late at night playing video games and slept his days away. He received warning after warning from his parents, and when he flunked his courses at the community college, a tough love ultimatum was given: Get a full-time job or join the military. Your choice, but in two months your room will be converted into a home office, and you will not be able to live here any longer.

At this time his part-time job had dwindled down to less than twenty hours a week, and he took no initiative in finding additional employment. He was well on his way to becoming a grown-up Peter Pan. About one week prior to the deadline, his mother sat him down and showed him some places (on the bad side of town) where he could possibly afford the rent. She reminded him that he would also need to pay for gas and car insurance and that his current income would not be able to cover the expenses. She then showed him the city bus routes and lovingly reminded him that the deadline to move out was fast approaching. It was the wake-up call he needed, and within days he joined the military. I am happy to report that he is out of the house and on his way to becoming a grown-up. My friend shed many tears along the way, wondering if she had done the right thing. I can almost assure you that had she not taken a tough-love approach, her son would likely still be sitting on the sofa, game controller in hand, surrounded by a sea of empty energy drink cans while his sweet mama prepared dinner in the next room.

As mothers, our hearts are wired to nurture and care for our sons. When they are young and utterly dependent on us to have their needs met, we feel a sense of value and worth. It feels good to be *needed*. We must remember that our divine call as mothers is to raise up godly seed for the next generation. And part of "raising 'em up" is to "move 'em out." Or "cut the cord," so to speak. It is unbiblical to allow our sons to remain dependent on us after they reach a reasonable age of self-sufficiency. It is God's design for boys to become men while under the tutelage of their parents. Our role is to guide them into adulthood and equip them with the tools and training necessary to survive on their own. The launch process begins when they are young and continues over the years. The assigned job for each mother is to raise her son to be a man, not a Peter Pan with chest hair who somehow never manage is to take flight beyond the Neverland of perpetual boyhood.

> *P*art of "raising 'em up" is to "move 'em out."

Dad:2:Dad

Go to VickiCourtney.com and click on the link to the 5 Conversations blog for my husband's list of activities and the books/training materials he has used with our sons to reinforce this conversation. While you're there, feel free to add your husband's ideas to the list!

Godly men are in short supply. Dare to become one!

CHAPTER 15

Wanted: A Few Good Role Models

*I*f you had to guess what makes the average teen/young adult (between the ages of thirteen to twenty-four) happy, what would you say? My guess would have been "hanging out with friends," "endless amounts of freedom," or perhaps "material possessions." When 1280 teens/young adults (between the ages of thirteen and twenty-four) were asked that open-ended question, believe it or not, the top answer was spending time with family.[1] This study, which was conducted by the Associated Press and MTV, also found that nearly three-quarters of young people say their relationships with their parents make them happy.[2] But that's not all. When asked to name their heroes, nearly half of respondents mentioned one or both of their parents. The winner, by a small margin:

mom.[3] Remember that one the next time you get an eye roll from your daughter or a door slam from your son.

In the book *Teenage Guys*, Steve Gerali says, "The first and most powerfully defining context for a guy is his family. Here he learns about gender roles, social expectations, and his uniqueness."[4] No doubt, fathers are of critical importance in a boy's life. Author and psychologist Michael Thompson notes, "A boy growing up without a male role model is like an explorer without a map."[5] Boys need to see how men act on the job and at home, how they handle stress, how they balance obligations, how they get along with family members, and, most important of all, how they plan for the future.[6] But what if a boy doesn't have the blessing of a father who lives in the home and is a godly role model? While the most ideal family dynamic would be a mother and a father who are happily married, following Christ, and raising their children to do the same, that is often not the case. In fact, it has become a rarity. Take for example Amy's challenge, which she details in an e-mail she sent me:

> My son is nine. My husband is an over-the-road truck
> driver, and he is gone a lot. My son loves his daddy and
> sticks to him like glue when he's home. But his daddy
> isn't a believer, and there is a shortage of positive male
> role models in his life. Out of a congregation of 250, only
> one of the men in our church is willing to work with the
> children on a weekly basis. What do you do when daddy
> isn't a believer, and there isn't a strong male influence in
> your son's life?

I have spoken with many mothers at my events that share heartbreaking accounts of husbands/ex-husbands who drink, swear, and/or engage in other immoral acts in the sight of their children.

Please know that my heart breaks for you if you fall into that category. I cannot begin to imagine the anguish you have experienced in not having the support of a godly husband and father to your children. If you face a similar challenge and your son does not have a strong male role model in the home, please do not despair. Whether you are a single mother or you are married to a man who is not a godly role model, please know there is hope. I commend you for picking up this book. It indicates you are the kind of mom who refuses to give up. You will have to work harder to expose your son to strong male role models, but hope is not lost.

While I cannot relate to your plight, know that I have kept you in my mind (and prayers) as I have written this book. I have tried not to make general, sweeping assumptions that most of the mothers in my reading audience would have husbands who are godly men, actively engaged in the rearing of their sons. The "conversations" I have presented in this book are grounded in one assumption: that mothers will share them with their sons, regardless of whether they have a husband on board to help them in that endeavor. Mothers who have the blessing of godly husbands who are on the same page may choose to delegate some of the more sensitive topics we have discussed to their husbands, but the important thing is that *someone* be willing to share the conversations. And share them often.

With that said, I would be remiss if I didn't share the importance of exposing your sons to godly male role models. Positive male role models (men committed to biblical manhood) are an important influence in the lives of all boys, including those who have been blessed with a godly father. Author John Eldredge says, "A boy learns who he is and what he's got from a man, or the company of men. He cannot learn it from any other place. He cannot learn it from other boys, and he cannot learn it from the world of women."[7] It is not enough for mothers to engage in the necessary conversations with their sons pertaining to their becoming godly men. Mothers must actively expose their sons to godly men who are "walking their talk" and "talking their walk." Coaches, scout leaders, etc., can be strong influences in a boy's life, especially if they model godly attributes associated with biblical manhood. This is especially important if you have a husband or ex-husband who is modeling *negative* behaviors that run contrary to God's standards for biblical manhood. As your son gets older, it may be necessary for you to acknowledge to your son the situation for what it is and express sorrow that he is missing a godly father role model. Pray about whether you should take this step. If you do, be careful not to bash his father but rather address the situation with a spirit of sincere humility. If you expose your son to godly men on a regular and consistent basis, your son can't help but draw obvious conclusions when it comes to what a godly male role model looks like.

It Takes a Village

Author Steve Gerali says, "From my observations guys tend to seek out male models on their own. They just gravitate toward them—it's a part of the internal mechanism of being a guy. Therefore, instead of finding a role model for her son, a single mother may need to be more concerned with helping him screen the models he's already pursuing."[8] As mothers, our job is to expose our sons to settings with a higher than normal concentration of men who are modeling biblical manhood. Send your son on church youth group or mission trips where godly male mentors are present. My younger son recently returned from a one-week mission trip, and in the course of telling my husband about the trip, he mentioned at least three adult men he spent time with that left a positive impression. "I really liked him." Or, "I didn't really know him before the trip, but he's so cool." Look for cues your son is dropping and send the men who have made a positive impression a thank-you note. I know these men are in short supply, but I can promise you they are out there. They are in your local churches, businesses, neighborhoods, and possibly on your own family tree. Author Rick Johnson advises, "Hold up male heroes for your son; he needs to see what they look like. Heroes need not be famous, larger-than-life action figures."[9]

If your son is not gravitating toward some of these men, there is nothing wrong with pin-pointing a few men you know (or have observed) who are exhibiting godly character qualities. In fact, we'll discuss some qualities in the next chapter that can help guide you. Once you identify a candidate, pray about the possibility of approaching him with a request to mentor your son. If God gives you a green light, move forward and express your desire to expose your son to an older godly man like him and see if he's interested.

Rick Johnson says, "Older men have a responsibility to walk alongside younger men, giving them the benefit of their experience. . . . It's important that you make these men aware that your son's father is not involved in his life so they will understand their importance in your son's life."[10] Who knows, you may be the conduit God uses to challenge the man you approach to become godly mentor. Remember, the benefits of a mentoring relationship are mutual. And do not be discouraged if you approach a potential mentor for your son and he declines the invitation. Stay the course. It simply means God has someone else in mind who would be a better match for your son. Trust God's guidance in your search.

Author Leonard Sax offers this wisdom: "To become a man, a boy must see a man. But that man doesn't have to be his father. In fact, ideally, it shouldn't be only his father. Even if your son has a strong father or father figure in his life, he also needs a community of men who together can provide him with varied models of what productive adult men do."[11]

My husband and I have intentionally exposed our sons to other godly men so they may see different personality types that share an equal and unwavering devotion to biblical manhood. Many of these men have become like second fathers to our sons and have played an active part in mentoring them along the way. A mother can teach her son about biblical manhood, but she cannot model what it looks like. I'm a big believer in the principle that "more is caught than taught." Therefore, it's crucial that our boys see a godly man up close and personal.

As mothers, our job is to expose our sons to settings with a higher than normal concentration of men who are modeling biblical manhood.

The Ultimate Role Model

Godly men are critical in our sons' lives, but the ultimate role model we should point our sons to is Jesus Christ. Even the best of human role models will make mistakes and at times disappoint, but Jesus never fails. While the trend of wearing WWJD wristbands may have expired, the question should never expire from our hearts. What would Jesus do? As our sons mature in their faith, the question needs to become a central foundation in their lives. In fact, if we followed any esteemed earthy role model for long, we would eventually become disillusioned. The apostle Paul reminds us of the appropriate hierarchy when it comes to following role models:

For when one says, "I follow Paul," and another, "I follow Apollos," are you not mere men? What, after all, is Apollos? And what is Paul? Only servants, through whom you came to believe—as the Lord has assigned to each his task. I planted the seed, Apollos watered it, but God made it grow. So neither he who plants nor he who waters is anything, but only God, who makes things grow (1 Cor. 3:4–7).

The best male role models are those who know their place—that of being a servant with an assigned task of pointing others in the direction of the only role model worthy of a following, Jesus Christ. While our culture is quick to prop up flawed celebrities, musicians, and sports figures, our sons need to be reminded that God exalted Christ to the highest place and gave Him the name that is above every name, that at the name of Jesus every knee should bow, in heaven and on earth and under the earth, and every tongue confess that Jesus Christ is Lord (Phil. 2:10–11).

CHAPTER 16

Raising Up a Gentleman

F ew people will ever forget the embarrassing scene onstage at the VMA awards show in 2009 involving Kanye West and Taylor Swift. If you happened to miss it, you probably heard about Kanye's deplorable behavior in the days that followed. He announced the nominees for Best Female Video, opened the envelope, and declared Taylor Swift the winner. He handed Taylor the award, and while she was in the middle of her acceptance speech, he proceeded to interrupt her, grab the mic, and rudely announce, "Taylor, I'm really happy for you, and I'm gonna let you finish, but Beyonce had one of the best videos of all time."[1] Fortunately the consensus from the public was one of total outrage. Pop singer, Katy Perry, tweeted in the aftermath of Kanye's ouburt: "Kanye, it's like you stepped on a kitten."[2] You know it's bad when Eminem, who is notorious for a few public temper-tantrums of his own, weighs in on Kanye and says, "He shouldn't have done that, man . . . I mean, she's a little girl."[3]

The scandal called attention to a real and present problem among today's young men: The traditional gentleman seems to be a lost and dying breed. The chivalrous, hat-tipping, surrender-your-seat-to-the-ladies brand of gentleman who courted our grandmothers is a long forgotten thing of the past. While I'm not suggesting we retreat back fifty years and start a hat-tipping revival, I do think parents need to be more purposeful when it comes to raising their sons to be gentlemen. In this chapter I want to address several key qualities that find their roots in the Bible and are necessary character qualities for every gentleman in training.

A Gentleman Values His Reputation

> A good name is more desirable than great riches; to be esteemed is better than silver or gold. (Prov. 22:1)

Often when speaking to teens, I challenge them with the question, "Are you the type of person who has a reputation?" The question makes some of them fidget a bit in their seats. If you looked up the word *reputation* in the dictionary, you might find this definition: "The generally accepted estimation of somebody; character, standing, name."[4] The truth is, each of us has a reputation a "generally accepted estimation" as determined by others. And that estimation can be overall good or bad. In order to illustrate the power of this "estimation" factor when determining a person's reputation, I tell my young audience that I'm going to announce several well-known celebrities, and when I do, I want them to think of one or two words to describe the person (to themselves, of course). I toss out names like Britney Spears, Tom Cruise, Lindsey Lohan, Chris Brown, and Miley Cyrus. I think you can imagine some of the words they come up with to describe these celebrities. I then make the point that they just branded each person with a designated reputation based on the public's "generally accepted estimation." I point out that even though they are not famous and in the public eye, they still are being "estimated" by others on a daily basis. I then challenge them to think of one or two words others who know them might use to describe their character if asked. Certainly it's an unsettling thought for some. I imagine I would have been among the "unsettled" had I been challenged by that thought at their age.

I once heard a speaker say, "You are who you've been becoming." Wow, what a powerful statement. Our sons need to know that you are judged by your actions. In my years of working with teen and college girls, I have had a good number cry on my shoulder over actions that have left them with tainted reputations. As we discussed in conversation 2, it is fairly common for children and teens to have a cognitive disconnect when it comes to making choices. In other words, it is difficult for them to mentally walk a decision down its logical path and weigh the possible consequences of the decision. Most of us likely can relate to that challenge during our adolescent and teen years and have our own fair share of negative consequences we tallied up as a result. However, this is where we must be faithful in helping our sons see that their actions determine their character, and their character, in turn, determines their reputation.

Socrates, the Greek philosopher from fourth-century BC, once said, "Regard your good name as the richest jewel that can possibly be possessed. The way to gain a good reputation is to endeavor to be what you desire to appear."[5] This is a difficult challenge for our children who are growing up in an age where the Internet records every step of their youth and forgets nothing. We must be diligent in sharing the key to obtaining a good reputation with our sons. It can be found in Proverbs 3:1–4: "My son, do not forget my teaching, but keep my commands in your heart, for they will prolong your life many years and bring you prosperity. Let love and faithfulness never leave you; bind them around your neck, write them on the tablet of your heart. Then you will win favor and a good name in the sight of God and man." In order to remember God's teaching, our sons must first know God's teaching. Upon knowing it, they must tuck it away in their hearts and pull from that reserve when the need arises. This is the point of impact when God's standard goes beyond simple head knowledge and takes root in the heart. We can do our part to provide them with adequate teaching over the years, but we cannot make them treasure that teaching in their hearts. Furthermore we cannot make them draw upon those truths and apply them to their daily lives. We can, however, pray like crazy from the sidelines.

> *In order to remember God's teaching, our sons must first know God's teaching.*

A Gentleman Is Chivalrous

While recently trying on some jeans at a nearby store, I couldn't help but overhear a conversation between two young women in the dressing room next to me. One of them was sharing a concern with her friend about her boyfriend's lack of good manners. "He just doesn't seem to get it. When we first starting going out, he paid for my meals, but now that we've been together for six months, sometimes he expects me to pay! And he's never once opened a door for me or waited for me to enter a place in front of him. The other day we were headed into the student center, and he walked into the building right in front of me while I was digging in my purse for my student ID, and he just let the door close behind him."

By this time it was all I could do to keep from screaming, "Dump him, sister! He's a dud!" As if her plight wasn't sad enough, wait until you hear her friend's response! "Yeah, but pretty much no guy opens doors anymore. I mean, I wish they would, but we can't blame them if they're not raised that way." It certainly inspired me to sit both my boys down in the days that followed and make sure they are behaving like the gentlemen their father and I raised them to be. Clearly chivalry is on the list of endangered character qualities at risk for extinction. Author Rick Johnson says, "Boys need to be taught to respect women of all ages—girls to grandmothers. They should open doors and carry heavy items for them, not because women are weaker or incapable, but because they deserve to be honored and cherished."[6] He goes on to offer the following advice to mothers of sons: "Teach your boy at a young age to open the door for you and for his sisters. As courtesy and respect manifest themselves in other areas of his life, they will become a lifelong habit and will help create an attitude that some future young lady will greatly appreciate and praise you for."[7] I imagine my neighbors in the dressing room would have shouted out a hearty "amen!" upon hearing that bit of advice.

Chivalry is controversial given the women's movement and the residue of confusion it left in its wake. While some women may find it offensive that a man would have the nerve to hold the door for them, the majority of women still welcome the gesture of kindness.

(And I doubt these feminists would dare to complain if they were on a sinking ship and a gentleman offered to give up his seat on the lifeboat to one of them.) Chivalry shouldn't be reserved for just women. Our sons should be taught to keep an eye out for anyone in need, including children and the elderly, and extend a helping hand should the opportunity arise. The wisdom of Luke 6:31 is timeless for every generation: "Do to others as you would have them do to you."

> *O*ur sons should be taught to keep an eye out for anyone in need.

Chivalry in Dating

While we're addressing the topic of chivalry, I want to touch on dating. I mentioned in chapter 14 that my husband and I have discouraged our children from dating recreationally and encouraged them instead to date with marriage in mind. The concept of dating with marriage in mind is fairly radical when compared to the mind-set most young people have when it comes to dating. Most young people today move too quickly into dating relationships and view dating as a follow-up to an initial spark of attraction to explore future compatibility. Rather than use dating as a forum to get to know someone after an initial attraction (the culture's model), when you date with marriage in mind, you spend a great deal of time on the front end getting to know the other person as a friend before deciding whether to move forward and date. When you choose to date with marriage in mind, you elevate the stage of dating to a more serious commitment that more closely resembles a preengagement period.

My husband and I have not been hard-core in our approach to dating, but we have been blunt about our views and expectations with our children. Even though we prefer our children date with marriage in mind, they have had a handful of dating experiences that didn't match that description. Regardless, my husband and I were actively engaged in monitoring those relationships and guiding them along the way. Fortunately our children did not date until later than the norm (our older two were seniors in high school), and in total there have only been a handful of dating relationships to monitor. (Each of our children spent about three to six months of their entire four years of high school in a dating relationship.) In the end God used those experiences to help them come to some wise conclusions on their own about dating and build a case for dating with marriage in mind.

All three of our children viewed dating with marriage in mind. Consequently they view dating as a serious step—a step you take when you feel you may have possibly met the person God is leading you to marry. For example, my daughter did not date her freshman year of college at all. She met a young man during the first semester of her sophomore year on a blind date through a friend. He was interested in getting to know her further (and vice versa) after the first date and asked her to go out to dinner the following week. After that date he asked her out again, this time for coffee. There were a few group activities mixed in with friends that followed and a handful of other dates. The more they got to know each other, the more interested they became in each other. In addition, many hours were spent on the phone getting to know each other better.

By the time they decided to formally date with marriage in mind, a period of four months had passed since the first date. They had spent those valuable four months getting to know each other without the physical and emotional complications/distractions that cloud most dating relationships. Therefore they were not at risk of basing a relationship on feelings or physical attraction. By the time they had decided to date, they knew each other's views on faith, marriage, and the things that matter most. Most important, they knew God was leading them to take the next step because they had cautiously and prayerfully sought His wisdom and guidance along the way. Her boyfriend had shared openly with her shortly after they met that he only dates with marriage in mind and that his goal was to help "guard and protect her heart" throughout the process that followed. (Certainly a godly and noble goal that put a smile on this mother's face!) In setting the standard up front, he showed many of the godly qualities we are discussing in this chapter. And I'm happy to say that this wonderful young man recently proposed to my daughter. I know this dating model sounds unreal, given the world we live in, but it is possible to date with integrity. And it is possible to raise our sons (and daughters) to date with integrity.

As mothers, we need to take the time to help our sons understand what chivalry in dating looks like. While I'm a big fan of kids hanging out in groups (especially, in the high school years), I think we need to be careful our sons don't come to rely on this model. We need to raise sons who know that part of growing up and becoming the men God intended them to be means putting the group dates behind them and pursuing a mate when the time is right. That means picking up the phone (please don't allow your sons to ask girls out via text message!), asking the girl out, driving over to pick her up, opening doors and displaying other acts of chivalry, picking up the check, and dropping her off at the end of the evening without expectation of a good-night kiss or anything more.

Dating doesn't have to emulate the world's model. In fact, if our sons are seeking to follow Christ, it shouldn't look anything like the world's model. If we say nothing about dating, our sons by default will conform to the world's model. Therefore we must include dating as an ongoing topic of conversation with our sons. I realize there are many different views of dating among parents who are seeking to raise their children to be godly. Please know I am not proclaiming the model of dating with marriage in mind as the one and only way to date. It has worked well for my children, and I've witnessed it work well for others. Again, my husband and I were not hard-core in our approach to dating, though we did have certain parameters (no dating prior to sixteen; no all-consuming, joined-at-the-hip dating relationships, etc.) All the while, we strongly expressed our position that dating be reserved for serious "marriage candidates." By allowing our children a little bit of freedom to give the world's model of dating a brief test-drive (under our watchful eye), each of our children in the end came to the conclusion that the world's model was faulty.

Dating doesn't have to emulate the world's model.

A Gentleman Is Selfless

Turn my heart toward your statutes and not toward selfish gain. (Ps. 119:6)

A true gentleman puts the needs of others before his own. Of course, this is a difficult discipline for our sons when they are exposed to a multitude of negative role models who glamorize selfish behaviors as the norm. While it's common to engage in an occasional narcissistic indulgence, for some self-indulgence becomes a year-round lifestyle. Take, for example, a recent study which found that college students are more narcissistic and self-centered than ever before. Five psychologists examined the responses of 16,475 college students nationwide who completed an evaluation called the Narcissistic Personality Inventory between 1982 and 2006 and asked for responses to such statements as: "If I ruled the world, it would be a better place," "I think I am a special person," and "I can live my life any way I want to." By 2006 the researchers found that two-thirds of the students had above-average scores, 30 percent more than in 1982.[8]

The study's lead author, Professor Jean Twenge of San Diego State University, said, "We need to stop endlessly repeating 'You're special' and having children repeat that back. . . . Kids are self-centered enough already."[9] The researchers attribute the upsurge in narcissism to the self-esteem movement that took root in the 1980s and further suggest that the effort to build self-confidence has gone too far. In the study Twenge points out that narcissists tend to lack empathy, react aggressively to criticism, and favor self-promotion over helping others. Not surprisingly, when asked to identify possible remedies to the growing problem, the researchers stated that "permissiveness seems to be a component" and that possible antidotes might include more "authoritative parenting" and "less indulgence."[10] It appears that narcissists are made rather than born.

There is nothing more unattractive than a person with entitlement issues. And yet I have to wonder how many mothers are feeding this monster, many through innocent attempts to boost their son's esteem. Oh sure, we need to cheer our children on as they discover their gifts and talents, but we go overboard if we are leaving them with the impression that they are somehow better than everyone else and deserve special favor in the world. Like when we question a coach's decision to put our son on the bench or in a position that doesn't "fully utilize his talents." Or march up to the school to fight their battles. Or allow them to sleep until noon in the summers and play video games all day without an obligation to get a job or chip in and help out around the house.

Then there are moms who feed their children the damaging lie that they can "be anything and do anything they want in the world if they just work/try hard enough." While it sounds nice in theory, it simply isn't true. Don't believe me? Just tune into the audition phase of *American Idol* to see this train wreck play out. Contestants who can't carry a tune in a bucket show up to audition, often with Mom by their side commenting off camera about how their child is destined for fame. How sad that a panel of strangers has to break the news to their child that he doesn't have the goods to be a pop singer! It's one thing to believe in our children, but we do them a disservice when we lead them to believe they are far more talented than they actually are.

Even if our sons have extraordinary talent, we need to make sure we don't build them up to the degree it lapses into an arrogant sense of entitlement. When my youngest played basketball his freshman year, a point guard on his team had amazing talent. Unfortunately the boy's parents had built him up to the degree he thought he was better than anyone else and, therefore, didn't have to play by the rules. As in, the *coach's* or *official's* rules. I remember sitting in the bleachers when an official gave him his fifth and final foul of the game. He shouted an expletive at the official before walking out of the gym (rather than back over to the bench to sit with his team). But what happened next said it all. His father flew out of the bleachers and headed for the official. The dad was up in the official's face, shouting, waving his arms and practically foaming at the mouth over the "injustice" done to his son. It's been several years since that scene occurred, and you might not be surprised to learn that this young man has had a whole lot of problems: bad grades (that prohibited him from playing sports), drugs, alcohol, car accidents, numerous accounts of disciplinary actions taken at school, time spent at the alternative learning facility, and the list goes on. He had the talent to play on a college team someday, but he may end up bagging groceries at the local supermarket down the road, if he doesn't end up in jail first.

Moms, if you have younger sons, pay careful attention to selfish behaviors they exhibit and, more important, your response to those behaviors. A sense of entitlement doesn't just happen overnight. It is bred into a child from his earliest days. Allow me to give you a case in point. Recently, while out to dinner with my husband, we were seated in a booth directly behind a family with young children. Halfway through the meal I couldn't help but overhear a disturbing conversation between the mother and her young son (who looked to be about four to six years old). To the best of my recollection, here is a script of their conversation:

Mom: Caleb, are you going to eat your fries?

Caleb: No.

Mom: Can Mommy have your fries then?

Caleb: *(pulling his plate closer toward him)* No, they're my fries.

Mom: But you said you're not going to eat them.

Caleb: Yeah but, they're mine. You can't have them.

Mom: Well, I don't think that's very nice.

That was it. End of story. Dad paid the bill and the family left with the fries still sitting on Caleb's plate uneaten. Honestly I don't understand what type of parenting philosophy (if any) this mother was employing, but if she gleaned it from a parenting book, she needs to burn the book when she gets home. In the situation I witnessed, there is a clear need for both behavior modification tactics and a frank discussion with Caleb about his sinful behavior and need for a Savior. Let's see if we can play this script out a bit differently:

> *A* sense of entitlement doesn't just happen overnight.

Mom: Caleb, are you going to eat your fries?

Caleb: No, they look yucky.

Mom: Can Mommy have your fries then?

Caleb: *(pulling his plate closer toward him)* No, they're my fries.

Mom: But you said you're not going to eat them.

Caleb: Yeah but, they're mine. You can't have them.

Mom: Caleb, let's take a trip to the bathroom.

(Conversation continues in the bathroom or outside the restaurant)

Mom: First of all, son, let's clear something up. Those fries aren't yours. Daddy and I paid for them, and, therefore, they really belong to us. For the record, the burger and the milkshake also belong to us, and your cozy bed at home, all your toys, your clothes, and even Domino, your pet hamster. If we decide we want them back or, better yet, we decide we want to give them away to another little boy, we can do that because all those things are ours.

Second, remember how we've talked about sin and how our hearts sometimes want to do the wrong thing? When you wanted to keep your fries even though you weren't going to eat them, that was selfish. Sometimes Mommy and Daddy are even selfish, but being selfish is always wrong. God is patient with us when we behave in a selfish way, but He doesn't want us to keep behaving that way. I know that sometimes it's hard to do the right thing, but when you think of how much God loves you and how He sent Jesus to die on the cross for your sins, like the sin of being selfish, then you want to do the right thing. Now, we're going to go back to the table and try again, OK?

Once back to the table, if Caleb doesn't surrender the fries to Mom, I would recommend that Mom enjoy the fries (and Caleb's milkshake!) while Dad takes over by removing Caleb from the table and employing a sterner form of discipline. Selfishness is a sin. How is Caleb going to recognize his need for a Savior if his parents sugarcoat his sin and allow him to continue in his sin with no consequences? Perhaps they'd be wise to remember Caleb will be the one caring for them someday when they're in a nursing home . . . or NOT, for that matter. If he's calling the shots in grade school, it's likely to get real ugly in the teen years! If we are to raise our sons to be gentlemen, we must nip selfish behaviors in the bud before they morph into a sense of narcissistic entitlement.

A Gentleman Is Humble

> Let another praise you, and not your own mouth; someone else, and not your own lips. (Prov. 27:2)

In my youngest son's junior year of high school, he and some of his football/basketball teammates started a Gentlemen's Day at their school. At one point my son referred to the group as the Junior Gentlemen's Club, but given that just about every strip club in America touts itself as a "gentlemen's club," I discouraged further use of that particular phrase! My son stated that the goal of Gentlemen's Day was to reinstate some of the old-fashioned gentlemanly qualities of days gone by. A mother could hardly argue with that. On the designated day Hayden dressed up in a button-down shirt and tie. I had visions running through my mind of these fine young men rushing to open doors for the girls, standing when their female teachers entered the room, and speaking throughout the day in standard gentleman dialect ("G'day to you, ma'am." "No please, after you." "May I carry your books to class for you, madam?")

With the toga incident (see chapter 2) still fresh in my mind, I wasn't entirely convinced their motives in instigating a Gentlemen's Day were altogether pure. Sure enough, my suspicions were confirmed when a fellow mother of one of the Junior Gentlemen got her hands on a picture that was taken of our group of boys while they were having lunch in the cafeteria on Gentlemen's Day. She e-mailed it to me, and I literally laughed out loud. Hayden and about six of his friends, each dressed in shirt and tie (some with jackets), sat around a lunch table they had covered with a white tablecloth. On the table was a burning candle centerpiece (isn't this a fire code violation?) and a couple of bottles of sparkling grape juice. My son was wearing a fake mustache while another young man had a pipe (minus the tabacco!) perched in his mouth. But perhaps the funniest part of the picture was the young lady standing off to the side (a fellow student they had recruited), who was serenading them with violin music as they ate their chicken nugget feast from their lunch trays and sipped their grape juice from their Styrofoam cups. Missing from the group shot of the young men celebrating the first official Gentlemen's Day? A little humility!

While the boys dressed liked a gentleman, they failed to heed the biblical counsel to "young men" offered in 1 Peter 5:5 and clothe themselves with the most critical item of apparel for every gentleman in training. "All of you, clothe yourselves with humility toward one another, because God opposes the proud but gives grace to the humble." Our sons need to know that the qualities that make for a true gentleman come from a heart that is submissive to God's leading. Only by His power are we able to quench our selfish tendencies and see others as more important than ourselves. Phillipians 2:3–4 reminds us: "Do nothing out of selfish ambition or vain conceit, but in humility consider others better than yourselves. Each of you should look not only to your own interests, but also to the interests of others."

Even though true humility stems from the heart, this doesn't mean we wait for our sons to come around on their own time and terms and practice humility when they finally *feel* like it. As with the other qualities we have discussed, we teach them spiritual disciplines at an early age and reinforce them over the years until they become second-nature. Our goal should be to raise our children to be Christlike. And when it comes to humility, Jesus is the ultimate example.

Your attitude should be the same as that of Christ Jesus: Who, being in very nature God, did not consider equality with God something to be grasped, but made himself nothing, taking the very nature of a servant, being made in human likeness. And being found in appearance as a man, he humbled himself and became obedient to death—even death on a cross! (Phil. 2:5–8)

> *We* teach them spiritual disciplines at an early age and reinforce them over the years until they become second-nature.

Humility is the opposite of pride. It is a constant reminder that we are "nothing" apart from Christ. Boys who learn to practice humility are better equipped to say no to sex outside of marriage, practice integrity in school and the workplace, feed the hungry and clothe the poor, make a marriage work, and overall behave in a Christlike manner.

Perhaps the best example we can leave with our sons when it comes to behaving like the gentlemen God created them to be is not an emphasis on an established code of moral conduct, but rather, allowing them to see our own personal example of a heart surrendered to Christ. We are servants and nothing more. Everything we have (possessions, talents, health, etc.) is by God's hand and belongs to God, including the wonderful blessing of our sons. They are simply on loan to us for a season. And that is certainly a *humbling* thought.

CHAPTER 17

Godliness over Goodness

*I*n this final chapter I want to speak to you candidly about the challenge to raise godly sons in an ungodly world. I want to come to you as a mother, not a writer with "expert opinions" (sorry, I'm not qualified!). Too often we pick up parenting books with the goal of finding some sort of tried and true formula for raising healthy and happy kids. You know, the kind of kids who grow up to say "please" and "thank-you," "yes ma'am" and "no sir." The kind who make their beds in the morning, share their toys with their siblings (without being told), and get gold stars on spelling tests. And when it comes to our sons, we want to raise them to be the kind of young men a mother points out to her daughter and says, "Now there's the kind of guy I hope you'll marry someday."

As our sons get older, we want to hear, "That's a fine young man you're raising."

Deep in our hearts we long to see evidence that we're on the right track with this parenting thing. In school and the workplace there are six-weeks grade reports and yearly employee evaluations to review progress and make any necessary changes along the way. Not so with parenting, which is why we have a tendency to gravitate toward how-to books, depend on occasional pats on the back, or even translate our son's successes as our own personal successes. Our sons are a reflection of us, and whether we want to admit it or not, we've all been guilty of trying to ensure that everything looks neat, tidy, and pretty on the outside. Some more so than others, but alas, we all lean in that direction. And let's face it, it's just plain easier to focus on the outside, where we can see evidences of positive change . . . and so can others.

The truth is we can train our sons to be chivalrous, polite, obedient, selfless, honest, and humble, but if their behavior is not motivated by a love for Christ and a desire to follow Him, they are relying on goodness rather than godliness. Isaiah 64:6 reminds us that our righteous acts are like filthy rags. But the sternest warning comes from Christ and His harsh words to the Pharisees: "Woe to you, teachers of the law and Pharisees, you hypocrites! You clean the outside of the cup and dish, but inside they are full of greed and self-indulgence. Blind Pharisee! First clean the inside of the cup and dish, and then the outside also will be clean" (Matt. 23:25–26).

Few would argue that many of our churches are filled with Pharisees who embrace a gospel of goodness over godliness. Admittedly there have been times when I've lapsed into that frame of mind. If we want to raise sons who are not only "good guys," but more important, "godly guys," we must teach them to keep "the inside of the cup clean." In order to do that, we must not shy away from talking about sin and God's redemptive story. Sin is not merely a behavior but rather a condition. Fortunately God provides a solution for our sin. It's our job to share the good news with our sons.

Getting to the Heart of the Matter

It's easy to focus on behavior modification strategies when it comes to training our sons in godliness. I've been guilty at times of focusing more on changing my sons' sinful behavior than encouraging them to turn to the only One who can change their hearts and their sinful behavior. And while I can manipulate my sons' behavior (at least at some level in the early years) in order to achieve a desired end result, I have no control when it comes to changing their hearts. Yet this is where true change must occur. Employing behavior modification strategies without addressing the heart does nothing more than put a BAND-AID on the problem. We must get to the heart of the matter.

Unless (or until) our sons are believers in Christ, their motivation and ability to change sinful behaviors will be rooted solely on their own human willpower. Yet for believers, true change occurs when our hearts respond to conviction of sin with a godly sorrow rather than a worldly sorrow (2 Cor. 7:10) and, as a result, turn from the sin (repent). The motivation to change is the unfailing love of God in that "while we were still sinners, Christ died for us" (Rom. 5:8). His kindness leads us toward repentance (Rom. 2:4)—the kind of kindness the father exhibited to his sons in the account of the prodigal son when he ran to him and greeted him with a hug and a kiss. No one and no thing can offer our sons that brand of unfailing love.

It's easy to react to our sons' sins with a set of swift consequences that discourage a repeat of the sins. However, we need to take the time to address the sins at the heart level in an effort to offer a permanent solution. We can't make our sons experience godly sorrow or, for that matter, even repent, but we can remind them of their need for a Savior and the price that was paid. When my youngest son leaves the house with his car keys in hand to meet up with friends, I used to yell out a last-minute reminder to "make good choices!" Now I yell out, "Remember the cross!"

> *We* need to take the time to address the sins at the heart level in an effort to offer a permanent solution.

One of the verses I often share when speaking at events is Psalm 26:2–3, "Test me, O LORD, and try me, examine my heart and my mind; for your love is ever before me, and I walk continually in your truth." We must teach our sons to lay their hearts bare before God on a regular and consistent basis. They are more likely to "walk continually in His truth" when they are in the habit of looking to God for an honest appraisal concerning the motives of their hearts. And of course, their motivation to stay on God's path is found in keeping His amazing, unfailing love ever before them.

Even Good Guys Do Ungodly Things

Some months ago I received an e-mail from a mother who was distraught to learn that her daughter, whom she described as a "good, Christian girl" had had sex. Her daughter was a junior in college and dating a "good, Christian guy" who was in his first year of seminary. Her daughter was living at home, and the mother stumbled upon a note from GCG (good, Christian guy) that indicated they had had sex. She was devastated that this "future pastor in training robbed her daughter of her virginity." Her purpose for writing me was to ask if she should come clean and tell her daughter about finding the note and encourage her to break up with GCG. She included excerpts from the note as evidence that they had clearly had sex.

Strangely, when I read it, I walked away with a completely different impression of GCG. I was most struck by the sincere regret he expressed in the note that they had "slipped up." His purpose for writing was to let her know he had experienced tremendous conviction and, after spending time in prayer over their sin, had felt led to take steps "to guard and protect her heart in the future." Some of the steps he listed included weekly accountability to an older, godly man, not spending time alone together in their apartments when their roommates were gone, and spending some time reading God's Word together and praying. But what really struck me was the godly sorrow he expressed in the note over what had happened and, more important, his desire to get back on track in His relationship with God, both for his sake and for his girlfriend's sake.

So in a nutshell there was a sin (a wrong turn at the crossroads); there was conviction over the sin, ownership of the sin (on the boyfriend's part), and godly sorrow that followed; there was an immediate U-turn and new direction; and there was a plan in place (as a result of his initiative) to hold him further accountable in the future in order that he might "protect and guard her heart." And this mother wants her daughter to break up with this guy? Through her hurt and disappointment over the loss of her daughter's virginity (by her daughter's own choice), this mother had failed to see that even though this good, Christian guy did a not-so-good thing, he chose to respond in a good and, more important, *godly* manner. Because that's how good, Christian guys behave when they love Jesus and are doing their best to follow Him on a daily basis. Mom failed to see that sometimes good Christian guys and good Christian girls do, in fact, make mistakes. In the end it's the heart that matters most.

During the course of writing this book, my husband and I experienced a situation with our youngest son (a good Christian guy) who made a foolish choice with some of his "good Christian guy" friends from school. Suffice it to say, they got off track in their walk with the Lord. I know some of you mothers with younger children may not want to hear that good Christian kids do, in fact, sin because, like me, maybe you imagined that if you did all the right things (read the latest and greatest parenting book; take them to church every Sunday; raise them on VeggieTales and Psalty's Singalong; sign them up for VBS every summer; involve them in youth group at church; send them to Christian camps and events; sign them up for mission trips; etc.) that somehow you can protect them from making some of the same foolish choices you may have made. Sorry to be the one to burst your bubble. Those are all wonderful things; and, no doubt, you are making "holy deposits" along the way. However, your sons will not be exempt from saying yes to temptations and straying from God's path. I know this because I was once you. And when my children stray, I would somehow manage to blame *myself.*

Given our own sin nature, why are we always so surprised when our sons (who don't have our maturity or fully developed frontal lobes!) choose to sin? This question weighed heavy on my heart as Keith and I dealt with our son's situation. We worked hard to get to the root of the real issue: the why behind his decision to sin and, more important, the condition of his heart. Oh sure, there were consequences and privileges revoked, but we invested most of our time in helping our son better understand the principle of godly sorrow and true repentance. We reminded him of God's patient and enduring love for him, even when he behaves in ways that are unbecoming. And then Keith and I prayed that he would react with brokenness and godly sorrow. We knew that without brokenness and godly sorrow the root of the sin would not be addressed. We might be able to modify our son's behavior with stern consequences, but it would only solve the problem temporarily.

In the end God used the situation to grow our son spiritually. He later admitted it was a wake-up call to get his attention before he strayed too far from God's path. We have seen evidence of positive change on the outside; but, more important, we know God is at work in our son's heart. In spite of our best efforts, our sons (yes, even the good Christian ones) are going to sin at times. Just as we do. Part of being a good parent is to teach our children how to get back up when they fall down. Not pretend they never will or, even worse, pick them up and give them a quick brush-off before the neighbors see them. It's far more difficult to raise a *godly guy* than a *good guy*. And if we're honest, we also know it's far more difficult to be a *godly mom* than a *good mom*.

> *It's far more difficult to raise a godly guy than a good guy.*

Final Thoughts

As we wrap up our journey through 5 *Conversations You Must Have with Your Son*, I find it strangely ironic that it coincides with my older son's launch into adulthood (marriage, fulltime job) and my younger son's final months in the nest. Needless to say, I have written these conversations with a certain sense of urgency as the clock ticks louder and louder in the background of my own parenting journey, signaling the close of one chapter and the beginning of another. My youngest son's exit from the nest will mark my official entrance into the empty-nest years.

Ask my closest friends and they'll tell you—I have been all over the board when it comes to my feelings about becoming an official "empty-nester." My response depends on the day of the week (not to mention, the time of the month!) and fluctuates like the weather in Texas. On some days I'm so weary from the challenges of parenting, I feel like putting a countdown clock on my computer desktop. Those are the days when I talk big and say things to my husband like, "Wow, not much longer! We're almost there, Honey!" (I also hint that we should celebrate the occasion with a trip to Hawaii.) Then there are other days when I am caught off guard with a simple reminder of the fleeting time. Like when my husband and I were recently sitting in the bleachers watching Hayden play his last and final high school football game. Ever. Keith simply said, "All these years of sitting in the bleachers on Friday nights, cheering our kids on in their various sports—I can't believe it's over. I wonder what we'll do next year?" I hope reading that made you sniffle because it means you're normal . . . and you're a mother. For the record, it made me more than sniffle and left me on the verge of needing to run to my car for an impromptu cry-fest. Even worse, Keith's eyes filled with tears as he saw my eyes welling up, which made my tears come even faster. I know he is going to miss having his sons around to watch their favorite sports teams on TV or play a pick-up game of basketball on the driveway. Oh, they'll still come by the house, but they won't be staying . . . as in sleeping soundly in their upstairs bedrooms . . . until noon . . . and leaving their wet towels on the floor for me to pick up . . . Wait, how many days until I'm an empty-nester, again?!

As I reflect on the journey of raising sons, I am overwhelmed with gratitude for the opportunity to play any part in the brief season they have spent in my nest. It was always God's plan that they would someday leave the nest and take flight into the world. My assignment was simply to prepare them for the flight. I don't know where you are in the journey when it comes to preparing your son for his final flight, but I do know this much: You are an amazing mother. You wouldn't have stuck with me for this long if you didn't care deeply about becoming the best possible flight trainer to the nestlings God has entrusted to your care.

Can I give you one last bit of advice before we close? Take it from a mother who, by the time you read this, will have filled out her last and final set of back to school forms (hallelujah!); attended her last and final parent/teacher conference (whew!); and watched her last and final child walk across the stage for high school graduation (sigh). It's true what they say: TIME FLIES. It may not seem that way right now, especially if you have little ones who are hanging onto your shirttail as you read this and begging for your undivided attention. Before you know it, you'll be sitting in the bleachers for the last-ever ballgame or snapping pictures of your son with his prom date. Or even better yet, sitting on the front row of a church and dabbing your eyes as he exchanges wedding vows with the new first lady in his life. Take it from a mother who experienced all of the above in one year—the clock is ticking faster than you think!

That said, take the time to talk to your son . . . and keep talking through the years. I promise you, he's listening. Remind him that you aren't expecting him to be perfect and have the guts to tell him that you're not perfect either. Help him cultivate the habit of laying his heart bare before God on a regular and consistent basis. Model that a relationship with Christ and a life lived in response to what He did on the cross is where true contentment and joy are found. Tell him that at times we all have a tendency to play the part of both the younger brother (who strays) and the older brother (who stays, yet focuses on "goodness" over "godliness") in the account of the prodigal son. But don't forget to tell him that God's part never changes. He responds with unfailing love, regardless of which part we play. Tell him God is more concerned with his heart and having a relationship with him than merely his good deeds. And tell him that no matter what, you will never, ever cease to pray for him.

As mothers, we're never really out of a job when it comes to this parenting thing . . . even after our sons leave the nest. Our sons will still need us. They will need our prayers. On occasion, they will still need a bit of motherly advice and encouragement. They will need a few home-cooked meals after semesters of living on cheap pizza, energy drinks, and Ramen noodles. They will need occasional reminders to get a haircut or clip their toe nails (gross, I know, but do you want them to get married or not?!) And then the day will come when they will introduce us to a very special young lady. And another day when they drop off their own little nestlings for us to babysit! (If we're not too busy traveling the globe on one of our many footloose-and-fancy-free tropical vacations!) As my husband and I sat in the bleachers at our youngest son's last and final football game and again on the front row of the church as our oldest son said "I do" to his beautiful bride, I reminded myself that my job as a mother is not over . . . it's just different. The truth is, I don't need stadium lights and high school bleachers to cheer my sons on in the journey that matters most—becoming the men God created them to be. My sons may have taken flight from my nest, but they will remain forever in my heart.

Dad:2:Dad

Go to VickiCourtney.com and click on the link to the 5 Conversations blog for my husband's list of activities and the books/training materials he has used with our sons to reinforce this conversation. While you're there, feel free to add your husband's ideas to the list!

Notes

Chapter 1

1. 2010 FLOTV—"Injury Report" Sneak Peek, http://superbowl-ads. com/article_archive/2010/02/06/2010-flotv-injury-report-sneak-peek, posted on February 6, 2010.

2. "Dockers 'Men Without Pants' March to Super Bowl," http://www. adweek.com, posted on January 21, 2010.

3. James Poniewozik, "Dodge Charger, 'Man's Last Stand,'" http:// www.time.com/time/specials/packages/article/0,28804, 1960734_1960750_1960769,00.html, posted on February 7, 2010.

4. John Eldredge, *Wild at Heart* (Nashville, TN: Thomas Nelson Publishers, 2001), 6–7.

5. Dennis Prager, "Is America Still Making Men?" http://www.wnd. com/index.php?pageId=122350, posted January 19, 2010.

6. Dictionary.com Unabridged; Based on the *Random House Dictionary*, © Random House, Inc., 2010.

7. Elizabeth Wellington, "Men's fashion retail goes tough-guy, nothing metrosexual about it; So long, sensitive side," http://www.philly.com/philly/phillywomen/90068257.html, posted on April 7, 2010.

8. Ibid.

9. Ibid.

10. Lini S. Kadaba, "Manning up; As the testosterone turns: The new retrosexual gets that strong and gallant guy thing going again," http://www.philly.com/inquirer/magazine/20100407_Manning_up.html?viewAll=y, posted on April 7, 2010.

11. Ibid.

12. Peg Tyre, *The Trouble with Boys* (New York: Crown Publishing Group, 2009).

13. Ibid., citing M. Conlin, "Look Who's Bringing Home the Bacon," *Business Week*, January 28, 2003.

14. Albert Mohler, "Where Are the Young Men?" http://www.albertmohler.com/2010/02/09/newsnote-where-are-the-young-men, posted on February 10, 2010.

15. Rick Johnson, *That's My Son* (Grand Rapids, MI: Revell , 2005).

16. Study explores why boys are falling behind girls in school, http://www.physorg.com/news66925169.html, posted on May 15, 2006.

17. Ibid.

18. Polly Leider, "Why Boys Are Falling Behind; Doctors and Educators Pinpoint Reasons For Gender Gap In Schools," http://www.cbsnews.com/stories/2006/01/23/earlyshow/leisure/books/main1231713.shtml, posted on January 23, 2006.

19. Ibid.

20. Tyre, *The Trouble with Boys*.

21. Ibid.

22. Stephen James and David Thomas, *Wild Things: The Art of Nurturing Boys* (Carol Stream, IL: Tyndale House Publishers, 2009), 125.

Chapter 2

1. Meg Meeker, M.D., *Boys Should Be Boys—7 Secrets to Raising Healthy Sons* (New York: Ballantine Books, 2008), 122–23.

2. Ibid., 91.

3. Ibid., 123–24.

4. Nancy Chodorow, *The Reproduction of Mothering* (Berkeley: University of California Press, 1978), and Samuel Osherson, *Wrestling with Love: How Men Struggle with Intimacy with Women, Children, Parents and Each Other* (New York: Fawcett Columbine, 1992) as cited in Steve Gerali, *Teenage Guys* (Grand Rapids, MI: Zondervan, 2006), 244.

Chapter 3

1. Rick Johnson, *That's My Son* (Grand Rapids, MI: Revell, 2005), 49.

2. Stephen James and David Thomas, *Wild Things: The Art of Nurturing Boys* (Carol Stream, IL: Tyndale House Publishers, 2009), 119.

3. John Eldredge; *Wild at Heart* (Nashville, TN: Thomas Nelson Publishers, 2001), 13.

4. Meg Meeker, M.D., Boys *Should Be Boys—7 Secrets to Raising Healthy Sons* (New York: Ballantine Books, 2008), 46.

5. Ibid., 49.

6. Rick Johnson, *That's My Son.*

7. John Eldredge, *Wild at Heart.*

8. Meg Meeker, M.D., *Boys Should Be Boys*, 33.

9. John Eldredge, *Wild at Heart*, 5.

Chapter 4

1. Nancy Gibbs, *The Growing Backlash Against Overparenting*, http://www.time.com/time/nation/article/0,8599,1940395,00.html, posted on November 20, 2009.

2. Ibid.

3. Ibid.

4. Ibid.

5. Rick Johnson, *That's My Son* (Grand Rapids, MI: Revell, 2005), 105.

Chapter 5

1. Kim Painter, "Your Health: Teens Do Better with Parents Who Set Limits," *USA Today*, http://www.usatoday.com/news/health/painter/2010-02-08-yourhealth08_ST_N.htm, updated February 7, 2010.

2. Peter Bearman, Hannah Bruchner, B. Bradford Brown, Wendy Theobald, Susan Philliber, *Peer Potential: Making the Most of How Teens Influence Each Other* available from the National Campaign to Prevent Teen Pregnancy, 2100 M St., NW, Ste. 300, Washington, DC 20037, www.teenpregnancy.org, cited in Anita M. Smith, *The Power of Peers*, http://www.youthdevelopment.org/articles/fp109901.htm.

3. Ibid.

4. Meg Meeker, M.D., *Boys Should Be Boys—7 Secrets to Raising Healthy Sons* (New York: Ballantine Books, 2008), 190–91.

Chapter 6

1. "Teenagers Programmed to Take Risks; Risk-Taking Peaks in Adolescence, According to Scientists at UCL," http://www.eurekalert.org/pub_releases/2010-03/ucl-tpt032310.php, posted on March 24, 2010.

2. Peg Tyre, *The Trouble with Boys* (New York: Crown Publishing Group, 2009), 181–82.

3. Steve Gerali, *Teenage Guys* (Grand Rapids, MI: Zondervan, 2006), 170.

Chapter 7

1. Ryan Singel, "Internet Porn: Worse than Crack?," http://www.wired.com/science/discoveries/news/2004/11/65772, posted on November 19, 2004.

2. "Hijacking the Brain—How Pornography Works," www.AlbertMohler.com, posted on February 1, 2010.

3. Paul Knight, "Teen Porn 101," http://www.houstonpress. com/2010-02-18/news/teen-porn-101, posted on February 18, 2010.

4. Patricia M. Greenfield, "Inadvertent Exposure to Pornography on the Internet: Implications of Peer-to-Peer File-Sharing Networks for Child Development and Families," *Applied Developmental Psychology* 25 (2004), 745–46, as cited in Meg Meeker, M.D., *Boys Should Be Boys—7 Secrets to Raising Healthy Sons* (New York: Ballantine Books, 2008), 65–66.

5. Ibid.

6. R. Albert Mohler Jr., "Pornified American—The Culture of Pornography," *Commentary by R. Albert Mohler Jr.*, August 22, 2005, as cited in Steve Gerali, *Teenage Guys* (Grand Rapids, MI: Zondervan, 2006), 88.

7. William M. Struthers, "This Is Your Brain on Porn," Youthworkerjournal.com.

8. Ibid.

9. "Hijacking the Brain—How Pornography Works," www. AlbertMohler.com, posted on February 1, 2010.

10. JUJU Chang and Vanessa Weber, "Hiding a Porn Habit Is Part of the Thrill for Many Addicts," Abcnews.com, posted on September 8, 2008.

11. Ibid.

12. Struther, "This Is Your Brain on Porn," Youthworker journal.com.

13. Ibid.

14. Mohsen Janghorbani and Tai Lam, "Sexual Media Use by Young Adults in Hong Kong: Prevalence and Associated Factors," *Archives of Sexual Behavior*, vol. 32, 2003, 545–53. Richters, Grulich, deVisser, and associates, "Sex in Australia: Autoerotic, Esoteric, and Other Sexual Practices Engaged in by a Representative Sample of Adults," *Australia and New Zealand Journal of Public Health*, vol. 27, 2003, 180–90, and a nonscientific survey by NOW, a Toronto lifestyle magazine, www. nowtoronto.com/minisites/loveandsex/2006/survey.cfm as cited in Leonard Sax, M.D., Ph.D., *Boys Adrift* (New York: Basic Books, 2009), 132.

15. Rick Johnson, *That's My Son* (Grand Rapids, MI: Revell, 2005).

16. "Hijacking the Brain—How Pornography Works," www. AlbertMohler.com, posted on February 1, 2010.

17. Marnia Robinson, "Unexpected Lessons fron Porn Users," www. PsychologyToday.com, posted on October 7, 2009.

18. Ibid.

19. Betsy Hart, "Give Sons a 'Porno Pep Talk,'" http://www.suntimes. com/lifestyles/betsyhart/2108852,ESY-News-EasyHart18.article, posted on March 18, 2010.

Chapter 8

1. Joe S. McIlhaney, MD and Freda McKissic Bush, M.D., *Hooked* (Chicago, IL: Northfield Publishing, 2008).

2. Ibid.

3. Ibid.

4. Gary and Carrie Oliver, *Raising Sons and Loving It!* (Grand Rapids, MI: Zondervan, 2000, 66, as cited in Rick Johnson, *That's My Son* (Grand Rapids, MI: Revell, 2005), 27.

5. Kevin Leman, *Making Sense of the Men in Your Life* (Nashville: Thomas Nelson, 2001), 130, as cited in Johnson, *That's My Son*, 68.

6. Johnson, *That's My Son*, 66.

7. Pam Stenzel, *Sex Has a Price Tag: Discussions About Sexuality, Spirituality, and Self-Respect* (Grand Rapids, MI: Zondervan, 2003).

8. Johnson, *That's My Son*, 68.

9. "Two-thirds of teens who had sex wish they had waited," http:// www.bpnews.net/bpnews.asp?ID=17294, posted on December 18, 2003.

10. "Sex Education: Start Discussions Early," MayoClinic.com, http:// www.mayoclinic.com/health/sex-education/HQ00547.

11. Kristen Zolten, M.A., and Nicholas Long, Ph.D., "Talking to Children About Sex," Center for Effective Parenting, 1997, http://www. parenting-ed.org/handout3/General%20Parenting%20Information/sex. htm, as cited in Johnson, *That's My Son*.

12. Johnson, *That's My Son*.

Chapter 9

1. "CDC Report Looks at Trends in Teen Sexual Behavior; Attitudes Toward Pregnancy," National Center for Health Statistics, http://www.cdc.gov/media/pressrel/2010/r100602.htm.

2. "Youth Risk Behavior Surveillance System—National College Health Risk Behavior Survey," 1995.

3. Sharon Jayson, "Most Americans Have Had Premarital Sex, Study Finds," *USA Today*, http://www.usatoday.com/news/health/2006-12-19-premarital-sex_x.htm, posted on December 19, 2006.

4. Ibid.

5. The National Campaign survey questioned 1,000 young people ages 12–19 and 1,008 adults age 20 and older, according to the news release. The telephone surveys were conducted by International Communications Research in August and September 2003. Founded in 1996, National Campaign is a private nonprofit organization with the goal of reducing the teen pregnancy rate by one-third between 1996 and 2005, www.teenpregnancy.org.

6. David Larson and Mary Ann Mayo, "Believe Well, Live Well," Family Research Council (1994).

7. David B. Larson, M.D., NMSPH, et al, "The Costly Consequences of Divorce: Assessing the Clinical, Economic, and Public Health Impact of Marital Disruption in the United States" (Rockville, MD: National Institute for Healthcare Research, 1994), 84–85.

8. Edmund T. Eddings, "Sexual Health Care: It's Important for Guys, Too," http://www.mtv.com/onair/ffyr/protect/sexetc_january.jhtml. Edmund T. Eddings of East Orange, New Jersey, is an editor for SEX, ETC., the national newsletter and Web site written by teens, for teens, on sexual health issues, published by the Network for Family Life Education at Rutgers, The State University of New Jersey.

9. "1 in 4 Teen Girls Has Sexually Transmitted Disease," http://www.msnbc.msn.com/id/23574940, posted on March 11, 2008.

10. Ibid.

11. Peter Jaret, "The 6 Most Common STDs in Men," http://men.webmd.com/guide/6-most-common-std-men.

12. Pam Stenzel, *Sex Has a Price Tag: Discussions About Sexuality, Spirituality, and Self-Respect* (Grand Rapids, MI: Zondervan, 2003), 51.

13. Ibid.

14. Ibid.

15. K. Christensson et al., "Effect of Nipple Stimulation on Uterine Activity and on Plasma Levels of Oxytocin in Full Term, Healthy, Pregnant Women," *Acta Obstetricia et Gynecologica Scandinavia* 68 (1989): 205–10; Larry J. Young and Zuoxin Wang, "The Neurobiology of Pair Bonding," *Nature Neuroscience* 7, no. 10. (October 2004): 1048–54; K. M. Kendrick, "Oxytocin, Motherhood, and Bonding," *Experimental Physiology* 85 (March 2000): 111S–124S, as cited in "Unprotected: A Campus Psychiatrist Reveals How Political Correctness in Her Profession Endangers Every Student."

16. Michael Kosfeld, et al., "Oxytocin Increases Trust in Humans," *Nature* 435 (June 2005): 673.

17. "The Benefits of Chastity before Marriage," http://www. foreverfamilies.net/xml/articles/benefitsofchastity.aspx.

18. Meg Meeker, M.D., *Boys Should Be Boys—7 Secrets to Raising Healthy Sons* (New York: Ballantine Books, 2008), 67

19. Joe S. McIlhaney, M.D., and Freda McKissic Bush, M.D., *Hooked* (Chicago, IL: Northfield Publishing, 2008).

20. A. Aron, H. Fisher, et al., (2005), "Reward, Motivation, and Emotional Systems Associated with Early-Stage Intense Romantic Love," *Journal of Neurophysiology* 94 (1): 327–37.

21. J. R. Kahn, K. A. London, "Premarital Sex and the Risk of Divorce," *Journal of Marriage and the Family* 53 (November 1991): 845–55. T. B. Heaton, "Factors Contributing the Increasing Marital Stability in the United States," *Journal of Family Issues*, vol. 23 no. 3, April 2002, 392–409.

22. McIlhaney and Bush, *Hooked*.

Chapter 10

1. Alan Guttmacher Institute in New York.

2. The National Campaign to Prevent Teen Pregnancy.

3. Neil Howe, William Strauss, and R. J. Matson, *Millenials Rising: The Next Great Generation,* (New York: Vintage Books, 2000), 200.

4. National Longitudinal Survey on Adolescent Health from interviews with more than three thousand pairs of mothers and their teens. The findings were reported by University of Minnesota researchers and in the *Journal of Adolescent Health,* http://mentalhealth. about.com/library/sci/0902/blteensex902.htm.

5. Diana Jean Schemo, "Mothers of Sex-Active Youths Often Think They're Virgins," *The New York Times,* http://www.nytimes. com/2002/09/05/national/05SEX.html

6. Jane E. Brody, "Teenage Risks, and How to Avoid Them," http:// www.nytimes.com/2007/12/18/health/18brod.html?pagewanted=1&_ r=1&ref=science?_r, posted on December 18, 2007.

7. Hanna Rosin, Even Evangelical Teens Do It: How Religious Beliefs Do and Don't Influence Sexual Behavior," http://www.slate.com/ id/2167293, posted May 30, 2007. (From the original study *Forbidden Fruit: Sex & Religion in the Lives of American Teenagers* by Mark Regnerus, a professor of sociology at the University of Texas at Austin. The book is a serious work of sociology based on several comprehensive surveys of young adults, coupled with in-depth interviews.

8. Ibid.

9. Diana Jean Schemo, "Mothers of Sex-Active Youths Often Think They're Virgins," http://www.nytimes.com/2002/09/05/national/05SEX. html.

10. Rosin, "Even Evangelical Teens Do It," http://www.slate.com/ id/2167293, posted on May 30, 2007.

11. "Taking the Pledge," CBSnews.com, http://www.cbsnews.com/ stories/2005/05/20/60minutes/main696975_page2.shtml, posted on May 22, 2005.

12. Ibid.

13. The Heritage Foundation, "Abstinence Statistics & Studies: Teen Virginity Pledges Lead to Better Life Outcomes, Study Finds," http:// www.abstinence.net/library/index.php?entryid=1396, posted September 21, 2004.

14. Ibid.

15. Ibid.

16. Bernadine Healy, M.D., "7 Factors That Foster Teen Virginity, Pledge or No Pledge," *U.S. News*, December 30, 2008.

17. Ibid.

18. Ibid.

19. See http://www.girlsaskguys.com/Sexuality-Questions/248240-should-i-feel-terrible-for-being-a-21-year-old.html.

20. Ibid.

21. Sharon Jayson, "Truth about Sex: 60% of Young Men, Teen Boys Lie about It," *USA Today*, January 26, 2010. Survey originally in *Seventeen* magazine.

22. Ibid.

23. Pam Stenzel, *Sex Has a Price Tag: Discussions About Sexuality, Spirituality, and Self-Respect* (Grand Rapids, MI: Zondervan, 2003), 36–37.

Chapter 11

1. "Many Teens Regret Having Sex; New Poll also Shows Parents More Influential than Friends or the Media," http://www.icrsurvey.com/Study.aspx?f=NatCam_Teens_Regret.html, posted June 30, 2000.

2. Joan Jacobs Brumbert, *The Body Project: An Intimate History of American Girls* (New York: Vintage Books, 1998), 204.

3. "Many Teens Regret Having Sex," http://www.icrsurvey.com/Study.aspx?=NatCam_Teens_Regret.html, posted June 30, 2000.

Chapter 12

1. Leonard Sax, M.D., Ph.D., *Boys Adrift* (New York: Basic Books, 2009), 134.

2. See http://www.johnnylechner.com/home.htm.

3. "Youth No Longer Defined by Chronological Age; Consumers Stay 'Younger' Longer," "Golden Age of Youth" study from Viacom Brand Solutions International (VBSI), http://www.marketingcharts.com/topics/asia-pacific/youth-no-longer-defined-by-chronological-age-35-is-new-18-6530.

4. Ibid.

5. Lev Grossman, "Grow Up? Not So Fast," http://www.time.com/

time/magazine/article/0,9171,1018089-10,00.html#ixzz0sXQDW1pX, posted on January 16, 2005.

6. Ibid.

7. Patricia Cohen, "Long Road to Adulthood Is Growing Even Longer," http://www.nytimes.com/2010/06/13/us, posted June 12, 2010.

8. Sharon Jayson and Anthony DeBarros, "Young Adults Delaying Marriage," *USA Today*, http://www.usatoday.com/news/nation/2007-09-12-census-marriage_N.htm, posted on September 12, 2007.

9. Patricia Cohen, "Long Road to Adulthood Is Growing Even Longer," http://www.nytimes.com/2010/06/13/us/13generations.html, posted on June 11, 2010.

10. Marcia Segelstein, "Late Dates: The Dangerous Art of Marital Procrastination," *Salvo*, Issue 8 (Spring 2009), www.salvomag.com.

11. Ibid.

12. Wendy Shalit, *Girls Gone Mild: Young Women Reclaim Self-Respect and Find It's Not Bad to Be Good* (New York: Random House, 2007), 4.

13. Ibid.

14. Segelstein, "Late Dates: The Dangerous Art of Marital Procrastination."

15. "Sex Without Strings, Relationships Without Rings: Today's Young Singles Talk about Mating and Dating," *A Publication of the National Marriage Project © 2000*, www.marriage.rutgers.edu.

16. "Dating for a Decade? Young Adults Aren't Rushing Marriage," http://www.usatoday.com/news/health/2010-06-22-10yearcourtship22_CV_N.htm, posted June 22, 2010.

17. Segelstein, "Late Dates: The Dangerous Art of Marital Procrastination."

18. Ibid.

19. Frederica Mathewes-Green, essay in "First Things," August/September 2005, http://www.firstthings.com, as cited in Albert Mohler, "What If There are No Adults?," http://www.crosswalk.com/news/weblogs/mohler/?adate=8/19/2005#1346589, posted on August 19, 2005.

20. Ibid.

21. Jessica Bennett and Jesse Ellison, "I Don't," *Newsweek*, June 11, 2010, http://www.newsweek.com/2010/06/11/i-don-t.html.

Chapter 13

1. Jessica Bennett and Jesse Ellison, "I Don't," *Newsweek*, June 11, 2010, http://www.newsweek.com/2010/06/11/i-don-t.html.

2. Ibid.

3. Ibid.

4. Ibid.

5. Albert Mohler, "The Case Against Marriage," *Newsweek*, http://www.albertmohler.com/2010/06/25/the-case-against-marriage-courtesy-of-newsweek, posted on June 25, 2010.

6. Joe S. McIlhaney, M.D., and Freda McKissic Bush, M.D., *Hooked* (Chicago, IL: Northfield Publishing, 2008), 101.

7. Ibid., 101–102.

8. Ibid., 105.

9. Ibid., 104.

10. Wendy Shalit, *Girls Gone Mild: Young Women Reclaim Self-Respect and Find It's Not Bad to Be Good* (New York: Random House, 2007), 19.

11. *Sex without Strings, Relationships without Rings: Today's Young Singles Talk about Mating and Dating*, A Publication of the National Marriage Project © 2000, www.marriage.rutgers.edu.

12. Pamela Smock, a family demographer at the University of Michigan, says about 70 percent of those who get married lived together first. "Cohabitation is continuing to grow, and it's become the model way of life."

13. *Sex without Strings, Relationships Without Rings: Today's Young Singles Talk About Mating and Dating.*

14. The National Marriage Project's Ten Things to Know Series, "The Top Ten Myths of Marriage" (March 2002); Alfred DeMaris and K. Vaninadha Rao, "Premarital Cohabitation and Marital Instability in the United States: A Reassessment," *Journal of Marriage and the Family* 54 (1992): 178–90.

15. "Seven Reasons Why Living Together Before Marriage is Not a Good Idea," www.stcdio.org/OMFmarriage-ministry/7reasonwhy.htm.

16. "Sociological Reasons Not to Live Together from All about Cohabiting Before Marriage," http://www.leaderu.com/critical/cohabitation-socio.html.

17. Linda J. Waite and Kara Joyner, "Emotional and Physical

Satisfaction with Sex in Married, Cohabitating, and Dating Sexual Unions: So Men and Women Differ?" 239–69 in E. O. Laumann and R. T. Michael, eds., *Sex, Love, and Health in America* (Chicago, IL: Universtiy of Chicago Press, 2001); Edward O. Laumann, J. H. Gagnon, R. T. Michael and S. Michaels, *The Social Organization of Sexuality: Sexual Practices in the United States* (Chicago, IL: University of Chicago Press, 1994).

18. The National Marriage Project's Ten Things to Know Series, "The Top Ten Myths of Divorce" (April 2001). David Popenoe and Barbara Dafoe Whitehead, unpublished research by Linda J. Waite, cited in Linda J. Waite and Maggie Gallagher, *The Case of Marriage* (New York: Doubleday, 2000), 148.

19. J. Wallerstein, J. Lewis, and S. Blakeslee, *The Unexpected Legacy of Divorce: A 25-Year Landmark Study* (New York: Hyperion, 2000), xxvii.

20. Shalit, *Girls Gone Mild*. Fortunately, since 1976 a nationally representative survey of high school seniors aptly titled *Monitoring the Future*, conducted annually by the Institute for Social Research at the University of Michigan, has asked numerous questions about family-related topics. Robert Bezilla, ed, *America's Youth in the 1990s* (Princeton, NJ: The George H. Gallup International Institute, 1993).

21. Ibid., Shalit, *Girls Gone Mild*. "Marital Status and health: US 1999–2002," Report from Centers for Disease Control (2004). This study, based on interviews with 127,545 adults age eighteen plus, found that married adults were in better psychological and physical health than cohabiting, single, or divorced adults.

22. *Sex without Strings, Relationships Without Rings*.

23. Ibid.

24. Ibid.

25. Ibid.

26. Meg Meeker, M.D., *Boys Should Be Boys—7 Secrets to Raising Healthy Sons* (New York: Ballantine Books, 2008).

Chapter 14

1. Meg Meeker, M.D., *Boys Should Be Boys—7 Secrets to Raising Healthy Sons* (New York: Ballantine Books, 2008), 81.

2. Nicole Beland, "Babes in Boyland," *Men's Health* (October 2004).

3. Ibid.

4. Leonard Sax, M.D., Ph.D.; *Boys Adrift* (New York: Basic Books, 2009), 142–43.

5. Ibid.

6. Albert Mohler, "What If There Are No Adults?," http://www.crosswalk.com/news/weblogs/mohler/?adate=8/19/2005#1346589, posted on August 19, 2005.

7. Sax, *Boys Adrift*, 136.

8. Ibid., 155.

9. Ibid., 123.

10. Lev Grossman, "Grow Up? Not So Fast," http://www.time.com/time/magazine/article/0,9171,1018089-9,00.html#ixzz0tUmEBnvj, posted on January 16, 2005.

Chapter 15

1. Jocelyn Noveck and Trevor Noveck, "Poll: Family Ties Key to Youth Happiness," The Associated Press (August 20, 2007), http://www.washingtonpost.com/wp-dyn/content/article/2007/08/20/AR2007082000451.html.

2. Ibid.

3. Ibid.

4. Steve Gerali, *Teenage Guys* (Grand Rapids, MI: Zondervan, 2006), 208.

5. Stephen James and David Thomas, *Wild Things: The Art of Nurturing Boys* (Carol Stream, IL: Tyndale House Publishers, 2009).

6. Gerali, *Teenage Guys*, 244.

7. John Eldredge, *Wild at Heart* (Nashville, TN: Thomas Nelson Publishers, 2001), 62.

8. Gerali, *Teenage Guys*, 236–37

9. Rick Johnson, *That's My Son* (Grand Rapids, MI: Revell, 2005).

10. Ibid., 162.

11. Leonard Sax, M.D., Ph.D.; *Boys Adrift* (New York: Basic Books, 2009), 204–5.

Chapter 16

1. "MTV Awards: West Disrupts Swift's Speech," http://www.cnn.com/2009/SHOWBIZ/TV/09/14/mtv.music.video.awards, posted on September 14, 2009.

2. Ibid.

3. James Montgomery, "Eminem Weighs In on Kanye West-Taylor Swift VMA Incident," http://www.mtv.com/news/articles/1644231/20100722/eminem.html, posted on July 22, 2010.

4. "Reputation," Dictionary.com, http://dictionary.reference.com/browse/reputation (accessed July 22, 2010).

5. See http://www.quotationspage.com/quote/2871.html.

6. Rick Johnson, *That's My Son* (Grand Rapids, MI: Revell, 2005).

7. Ibid.

8. "Study: College Students More Narcissistic Than Ever," http://www.foxnews.com/story/0,2933,254904,00.html, posted on February 27, 2007.

9. Ibid.

10. Ibid.

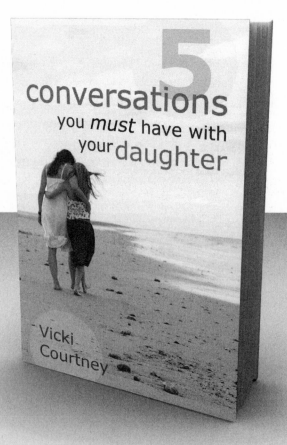

TODAY I PUNCHED JOSH AT RECESS!

BOYS WILL BE BOYS … RIGHT?
Millions of boys grow older, but very few become great, godly men. And with so many influences from culture, friends, and celebrities, how can you be sure which category your son will fall into? Prepare to talk to your son about the tough topics with Vicki Courtney's *5 Conversations You Must Have with Your Son: The Bible Study*. Because even though knowing what to say—or how to say it—can be hard, there's no one better to teach him about life, love, and faith than you.